The Downfall of Atlantis

A History of the Tragic Events Leading to Catastrophe

By Candace Caddick

GW00569763

Brightstone Publishing

First published 2011

Published by Brightstone Publishing
2 High Trees Road
Reigate, Surrey RH2 7EJ
United Kingdom

ISBN registered to me, the author, under Brightstone Publishing.

British Library Cataloguing in Publication Data
A catalogue record for this book is available from the British Library

ISBN 978-0-9565009-1-5

Printed in the United Kingdom

In appreciation for the help given to me by my two daughters,
Heather and Pippa Caddick

Books by Candace Caddick

Planet Earth Today: How the Earth and Humanity Developed Together and Where We're Going Next (April 2010)

The Downfall of Atlantis: A History of the Tragic Events Leading to Catastrophe (February 2011)

Contents

Acknowledgements

I would like to acknowledge the generous help I have received from members of the UK and worldwide Reiki communities. In particular the following Reiki Masters: Jean Jones for reading and commenting on the drafts, Kristin Bonney for her active support, and Phyllis Furumoto for her help and belief in me. Justine Sharifian has helped in every way. I am also grateful for the support of my husband while writing this book.

Introduction

I found writing this book a more visual experience than my previous book *Planet Earth Today*, which was written by listening to the Archangelic authors. This time the Archangelic Collective showed me scenes of them teaching, the beautiful white cities of Atlantis and the pits of horror below the temples during the Atlantean Fourth Age. The kingdoms of the Third Age were seen in levels of energy like the balls in Galileo glass barometers, some rising to the light and others falling into darkness. The sunlight gleamed from the polished wood in the tree cities of the North Atlantean civilisation-in-exile, the wood absorbing the sun and reflecting it back into the rooms. Guinevere sat in the forest silently, surrounded by her kin while working with Earth energy behind the front lines of battle.

The Fourth Age was based on a deeply cruel and horrific society and it was hard for me to watch, and harder to feel. Sometimes I would have to turn away and not write for a while. What happens to a living being's *soul* when it is cloned, and what happens to a society that is filled with these damaged individuals living on and on for as long as thirty thousand years? The cloning was the greatest cause of the genocide and slaughter in that Age. This was the era of wizards and magicians who cursed and destroyed lives and villages from afar, and the final Wizard Wars of Atlantis.

Atlantis may have existed for as long as one hundred and thirty thousand years. The post-Atlantean civilisations were also successful for at least fifteen thousand years before they began to deteriorate. If you consider an advanced ancient civilisation like Egypt, it was only the final rustic end to a civilisation of great learning and skill.

I was glad the Archangels decided to give more information about the great stone circles of Stonehenge and Avebury, and Glastonbury Tor. On visits to Avebury over the last few years I have watched the golden higher dimensional structures being built there as it prepares for what is coming next, and spoken with the stones about their roles in healing. The functions of the stone circles were once known to everyone.

In the final section there is the glorious and ongoing story of King Arthur, still remembered today. What exactly was the story of his life and death? I could see his small, serious face as he stood by his mother's side with the armies of the Shadow of the East just below the horizon, the black sky lit by flashes of light coming up from the hordes of soldiers. He sat in war councils and met Merlin, and for a brief time could be a boy again before taking up the role he was born to play. Merlin's final battle was similar to those of the Fourth Age of Atlantis; there were curses flying and magical defences. Arthur's is an unfinished tale, and the events have remained in our subconscious minds surfacing over and over again as background to more recent stories like Richard Wagner's operas *The Ring Cycle* and the works of J.R.R. Tolkien. For me, the selflessness of Arthur and the sadness of his story were the most touching parts of the book.

Section One

The First Three Ages of Atlantis

1

THE HISTORY OF the Fourth Age of Atlantis has been burned into the human consciousness. A few of the events covered in this book have been mentioned by other authors over the years, and part of the reason that so much has been written about the continent of Atlantis recently is our remembrance of those dark times. The memories that are surfacing now will take much of the rest of this book to explain. We hope that when you have finished reading you will be able to see the parallels in your modern society, and understand where similar actions have led in the past. We are writing this book in the name of the Archangelic Collective, and it is a book of light, written by angels of light. When you read this book remember that we were witnesses to all that happened in the ages of Atlantis.

Some of the introductory information here has been covered in greater depth in the previous book *Planet Earth Today*, written by the Archangelic Collective. However this book was written to be understood without reading the earlier book first.

When you look at the history of your race on this planet you must remember that you are the fifth race here to ascend to the light in partnership with the Earth, and that the events in Atlantis took place at the beginning of your time. Atlantis was devised so that you could play a great game to find yourselves as a tiny part of God, and when it failed you did not give up but continued searching. You are now within sight of the end of your quest, although it is hard for you to see it that way. We angels are here in force at this time to give help and assistance when you ask us for it. Many things are happening now to help you ascend, and to prove you are people of love. Despite your unhappy beginning in Atlantis you have come a very long way.

The downfall of that pleasant land began long before the start of the Atlantean Fourth Age. It came about due to part of the contract between the human soul and the planet Earth, a contract that veiled the higher dimensions from humanity while playing its game of discovery. This game was designed to teach the human soul about itself as an aspect of the Creator; you would look for God from a position of blindness and unknowing. Over the ages many of you have found and understood your role as a tiny part of God living in this universe; you realise you are God, and everything is God that exists inside this universe. This is the goal you are working towards on this planet while living your many lives.

Although it seems unlikely to you that the initial contract was flawed when it was drawn up, that is exactly what happened. On no other planet were the higher dimensions veiled from view of the local populace. That's because it is a very dangerous thing to do in a universe made up of light and dark, good and evil. It does not help for humanity to believe that there are only angels of light and no demons of darkness; after all you can see that there are both good and bad human beings living around you. You could see neither we who try to help you, nor those who prey upon you. When you began your lives in Atlantis many of you could see and hear us, the angels of light, and learn from us, just as today some can see and hear us. None of you could see the demons that wrap around and live off your energy, or influence your actions and lives, because they choose to work unseen. This was the crucial flaw in the way your game was set up; you could not see if you were in trouble yourself, or if you were dealing with someone who was a puppet.

Before Atlantean days people developed hunter-gatherer societies; and they migrated into the entire world, into new unpopulated areas. There were those who found the islands of Atlantis and settled there, where it was convenient for us to teach them because they were not migratory. We could teach sitting on a rock by the stream, and the parents would also teach the children. We would continue to teach the parents from generation to generation, and the population learned very swiftly that way, hot housing is a modern word for it. In the wider world we also taught, but often those people would move on and their lives were harder and more focused on basic necessities. It was much slower and more haphazard. We wished to tell people about their origins as children of the stars, about the universe they were a part of, and how they were beloved children of the light. We introduced spirituality and reason to them.

Atlantis in the beginning was a fruitful and pleasant land; peaceful green valleys surrounded by gentle hills. People had a hopeful and trusting nature and treated others, whether they were human or non-human, as they would wish to be treated themselves. This is the one rule of existence that matters across the universe, the only rule that will bring you closer to God. Treat everything with the respect you would accord your Creator if he or she stood before you, because that is who is standing before you in a disguised form. There is nothing that is not God, or a part of God. The new humans that lived in Atlantis in the early ages had not completely forgotten this rule and lived according to it.

Imagine a rural society, a Garden of Eden where all food was there for the picking and fish were plentiful. Humans had enough to eat always, and warm homes where heat and light were provided by the Earth herself through crystal energy. The source of the food and gentle environment was the planet, which had agreed to help the human soul reach ascension into light, and nurtured humanity with care. There was no need for harshness or a difficult environment for you to live in. Your lessons of ascension never required that you live in hardship while you learned about the nature of God. The new world created for you had everything you needed for life and pleasure, for joy is a favourite part of the Creator without which life is hardly worth living.

You lived by hunting and gathering, with song and story. The days went by easily and there was laughter under the star-filled skies at night. You looked into each other's eyes and saw shared humanity there, and treated each other with respect and kindness. We came as Archangels to walk among you and teach you about the greater truths of the universe.

What went wrong?

Now we come to the flaw that was written into the original contract between the human soul group and the planet Earth. You were unable to see the dark angels, or demons, when they clustered around you, or even feel when one would attach itself to you like a parasite. No one asked for it to leave or be removed by us, so it had successfully found its host body. These demons would influence the host by altering their emotions. Depression and joylessness are the first signs, followed by anger and cruelty, hate and the rest of your seven deadly sins. That was in the beginning, and now many of you have learned these behaviours by living in societies where a great number act as if they are controlled by demons. Back then it was assumed the person acting depressed or cruel was ill and they went to the healing temples, where help was available for them.

The demons never gave up; they saw this was a way to gain control of a planet, by gaining control of one of the dominant populations. There are two prizes to be gained here: one, and by far the largest, is the planet herself; the second is the human soul. So the demons set out to entwine themselves around as many as they could, especially by targeting those in power or respected positions. Some people resisted the darkness and hung onto their knowledge that all humans were one. There are many today who continue to resist and deny the demons a safe berth in their energy fields. These valued people are gaining in strength and numbers daily.

There are levels of influence and control that demons exercise when they have wrapped themselves around someone. Some people are woven in skeins of darkness and it can take a long time for every strand to be released. When they are freed they are themselves again and can use their energy for their own needs without sharing it with a number of freeloaders. For others it can take a long time to recuperate; they look like they are participating in life but are not wholly present, they have sustained such a high level of damage. These would have been helped in the healing temples in Atlantis, but now you do not remember that this could be a problem, or what a healthy individual is.

Today there are many in positions of power and influence that have these entities wound around them. Some find it easy to abuse their positions of responsibility because they are not wholly in control, and do not fight against what is happening to them. Others seem like hollow men, where the person seems to be missing from inside; these are puppets and very dangerous to you all. Somewhere inside of both these types the real person remains unseen and unheard, perhaps from birth to death. It is possible to rescue even these and restore their lives to them.

We are explaining this now, although it is a little scary, because it is part of your world and you can't see it, or very few can see it yet. It was the same in Atlantis, where a gradual takeover of the human population occurred and those with influence would be chosen and their behaviour altered. Now you have a new history where joy was to be deliberately destroyed, and a promising start to finding the Creator hijacked.

Your scientists recognise light in radio waves, televisions waves, electromagnetic waves and visible light waves. We include all that and more in our definition of light; we include love as our definition of the purest form of light. Love is how you feel light in your bodies, hearts and souls. Fear is the opposite of love, not hate. Hate is an emotion, a reaction, a fear-based belief system. You carry love in your person and it shows as light, it spreads outwards and lights the way for others. The absence of light creates darkness, which is how we define fear. Humans may feel darkness in their souls through fear. It is often caused deliberately through lies, and keeps humans subdued and frozen in place with no forward movement. It is a weapon being used against you.

In your Bible you have the allegorical story of the Garden of Eden, which showed a life of ease and simplicity. When Adam and Eve left the Garden they were cursed to bend and toil in the fields to grow their own food and their life of ease was over. If only you could all go back into the Garden and live in joyful ease again! We do not see why not. There are many steps along that road, but it is possible for humanity to return there one day. We hope that you will choose to do so and make the changes necessary to live in that way again in future generations.

Before we write any more about how you may return we will take you through a history of the sad continent of Atlantis and the early civilisation that foundered there.

2

ATLANTEAN SOCIETY existed for three long ages before it went dangerously wrong. During those three ages there was a defined shift at the end of each age. The first age was a gatherer society, with easy, happy lives. The human population slowly grew and the settlements were small; mainly composed of extended family groups. There was no winter, or drought, illness or decrepit old age, and the children were raised in love. The people lived long life spans that could be up to two hundred and fifty years side by side with their children and grandchildren. At this time they had not yet divided into male and female and their children were not brought forward with pain as women give birth today. They reproduced through love and the desire to have a child; it was all that was needed to manifest the baby onto the Earth from the higher dimensions in those days.

We did not see much progress in finding God, but neither did we see that this could one day go so wrong. We watched and guided in the early days, and our temples and meeting places were only clearings in the wood, or a large stone by a stream. No one needed anything grander than that, and would not have understood why a temple was built when there was no need for one. We would come to these places and teach those who came to learn from us. We taught them about the stars and the other planets, about angels and the elementals. Where you struggle to see a fairy or a centaur, they lived with them side by side. We shared with them the attributes of the light: truth, love and joy. These lessons they lived daily and we were pleased with their understanding and actions, but disappointed that the learning was so very slow.

The First Age continued for many thousands of years, with low population growth and a contented and simple society. At no time during the First Age did the people plant crops or toil in the fields, although they took to the oceans and fished for food. They created artwork, pottery, weaving and music, and educated their children to be proficient in all of these. Later on in other Ages there would be schools with reading and writing. The animals did not fear them nor were they eaten for food or harnessed to wagons at that time. People and animals were happy and lived joyfully.

There was a man, just one man in the beginning, who was living in a medium-sized village near a forest and a river. This was one of the areas where we had a clearing in the trees nearby to bring people together for teaching. This strong man, in the prime of his life, was a respected member of his community, and others often went to him for advice or help. (We say man here to help you understand, but of course it was a person of no sex whatsoever.) This man was out in the forest one day when he walked across a trap, made out of a higher dimensional nest of dark beings. He was not aware but he carried away with him members of that dark community in his aura fields (his energy bodies.) He returned to his village changed, and behaved differently to when he had left even though he looked the same.

Now when the smaller and weaker members of the village needed help they no longer received it from him. He found these people could be forced to help him instead if he hurt them, and made them afraid of him. When they brought back food they had to give some to him as well, an early form of tribute or protection money. By the time that man died over a hundred years later their society had

11

changed permanently to one that would be familiar to you now.

Unfortunately, he was not the only one who picked up entities. At this time others also came home changed in their moods and ideas; and they turned away from joy and set about creating fear and unhappiness in their villages for their own benefit. The other villagers worked harder to have enough food for themselves and to give to the chief. The earlier, easy society had changed into one where the mood and tone were different, setting up an energetic food supply of fear that strengthened the demons.

The end of the First Age is considered to be when joyful living left the people and their hearts were filled with sadness and fear. These were still gatherer societies, and the change to farming and toil would come in the Second Age. First let us consider the ramifications of the change from joy to fear and sadness.

When joy began to disappear from the hearts of the Atlanteans, they lost their connection to love and their hearts were filled with darkness. Their ability to discern truth was gone. It's still there, but truth is seen in the bright light whereas lies and deception flourish in the shadows. The filter that allows you to tell truth from lies became clogged with darkness and stopped working. A simple lie like "you need me to protect you from others" was suddenly seen as truth, and brought about new relationships within the community. That kind of lie only works where fear is present, and it is less easy to love when you are afraid of someone. Today these kinds of lies live on in the fear and lack of love for neighbouring communities, religions, and people. The lies are hugely expanded and woven into your societies, but you still have the light to help you discern truth. And we are happy to say it is a little lighter every day.

Truth was hidden, and joy and love were fading as a result. Distrust and lies multiplied and with their hearts blocked by darkness people had no idea how to proceed. They still lived in small and medium villages, but learning had ceased and there was little forward movement. Rivalries sprang up between villages and militia were trained for war. Those involved in protection for the village had to be fed by others who worked much harder than before. This led to such a profound change in the relationships between the villagers that strata developed with the stronger warrior caste on top. When joy is gone then love is reduced, and fear and cruelty thrives.

The way demons increase their numbers is to create the type of energy they thrive on, and then use that energy to multiply. The new village societies had been twisted to provide this type of energy for food; in particular fear. Fear, hatred, cruelty, and bullying all combined to produce the type of sorrow that fed the demons the best. We were looking at a new race of slaves, all providing energetic food for the invisible demons that were flourishing there. Demons are never kind to their hosts, and they took them deeper into misery to change the energy even more. Not everyone was susceptible to their influence, but those remained in the minority. The majority blindly accepted the lies that had been told to them about danger and scarcity, and prepared for tribal war.

It was about this time, at the beginning of the Second Age, that we took counsel and aligned ourselves with the ruling families of the main tribes. By choosing to work with the rulers we were fighting for the light on behalf of everyone who lived in the societies. We appeared as angels in human form, great beings of light. We established our healing temples where we taught daily, with the blessing of the leaders. Our temples allowed the light to be present and protected, and we saw with joy that the people still wished to connect with it. We began our teaching of Reiki so that each individual could maintain their connection to the light for themselves, no matter where they were. For a long time these steps pushed back the darkness and pain of separation from each other and the Creator.

At the beginning of the Second Age there were people living in small central cities, where they had control over the neighbouring villages. Farmlands were now in cultivation between the villages, created because it was easier to monitor the villagers, and easier to predict and tax the amount of food grown. The days of eating while wandering through shaded forests were gone, and the backbreaking toil in the fields under a hot sun had taken its place. It's not that humanity was thrown out of the Garden of Eden, but that they walked away following their leaders. After a while they thought that it was an improvement to grow crops; they had made progress and wouldn't want to go back to the lax, unstructured life they used to have. No one was alive who remembered what it was like to live that way, and they believed what they were told, that life was better now. The separation of the collective human consciousness, where each individual is isolated from one another prevents you from accessing the memories of your race. This was also a choice humanity made when contracting for this game. (The full contract is covered in *Planet Earth Today*.)

Over the years of the Second Age this agrarian society slowly developed, crops were grown, and there were weekly village gatherings where Reiki was channelled to the Earth in return for all she gave them. Healing sessions took place in our archangelic temples. We saw that happiness was present, but there was also a great deal of unhappiness and sorrow in the new lives. Fear and lies were the basis of the new societies, and decisions were based on these instead of what would make each individual joyful. This was how they lived across the land.

Life continued in this way through the Second Age with new trends developing; people lost contact completely with all those who were not from their set of villages, and to travel meant certain death or slavery. There were frequent skirmishes between nations looking for more land and slaves, and fishing boats went well-armed onto the sea to avoid capture. The people maintained their health through practising their own Reiki, participating in the village healing circles and trips to the temples. Dynasties formed and the caste systems became rigid with the peasants growing the food at the bottom. All this continued to seem normal to them.

This Age was the first one to produce people who became physically ill, and who had to receive many healing sessions in our temples before they were better. It was the beginning of a worrying trend where people abandoned responsibility for their own health, and looked to others to make them better and maintain their well-being. We did not understand this new attitude but found that the numbers of those who felt that way were increasing. Our temples became continually busy healing the sick. We saw the same people coming back time after time, and when they went away they still did not practice their Reiki daily to maintain their health because they wanted us to do it for them. Reiki was never meant to be something that was solely received from others; it was a gift for all to keep their connection to the universe, and to receive what they needed to stay in contact with the light.

The way of living changed during the Second Age from people who lived in ease upon an abundant Earth, to the majority of people toiling for their food. The food the Earth provided changed from a variety of forms to many fields of wheat grown to be pounded and ground to bake bread. Only the few people at the top had life easy any longer. Those who ruled never seemed to have enough, and their wants were never satisfied. Over and over again there would be raids against neighbouring villages so they could have more slaves and food, more than they could ever use. What difference did it make if they ate from a golden plate instead of a wooden one? How could their desires ever make up for the misery of separated families, either by death or slavery?

This became the whole point of the civilisations, to increase misery so that this would cease to be a planet of light, and the human soul would never reach ascension. The story of Atlantis is one of providing food for the dark angels in the form of pain and fear, and is one of great sadness.

Although the human population was ensnared in unhappiness, at that time there were many alive who had clear minds and understanding who were not contributing food for the demons. The light of love and truth remained strong in their hearts and they resisted until the end and worked against the lies. These people maintained their contact with the universe and love through Reiki and by not living in the centres of the cities, but out in the wilder areas. They maintained their contact with trees and animals, and the natural countryside. Some areas of natural beauty were so beloved that they could never be colonised or degraded. In your present day you still have areas like this available to you to visit or live in. When you go there you will find the Earth as she was in the beginning, alive with joy and generous in her being.

3

B Y THE END of the Second Age a rigid system of small kings and serfs was in place. We Archangels continued to come and teach in our temples, but few of the working people were allowed time to come. They needed no education to work in the fields. Instead we found ourselves counselling the rulers to try to ameliorate conditions from the top down. Sometimes this worked, but it depended on who was king at the time, and the next king could wipe out all the good done by the previous king. We continued our work and hoped we could use our influence to change the energy pattern back to joy. The Second Age ended with stagnant societies perpetually warring.

The beginning of the Third Age was marked by the winds of change blowing through these societies. Although not as bad as the Fourth Age became, the groundwork was laid during these times for what came to happen later.

The days of the city states were coming to an end, and the political groups grew larger to form small kingdoms with different languages. There was no longer frequent inter-marrying between them. The result was a great difference between the countries in the terms of light and dark. Some were home to vast healing temples and gardens where many variations and refinements were learned to maintain balance and health. In these countries, the people were treated more kindly and the rulers were not a burden on the populace. Today many of these practices are resurfacing, and you hear about them from those who remember being a priest or priestess in those temples. We approve of any form of healing that uses light and results in balance and inner knowledge. Many of these healing variations were inspired by us in their beginnings and some were immediately more popular than others. In these states we worked closely with the rulers and kings and the entire country rose higher and higher into the light, where wholeness and happiness of all the people were the most noticeable features.

Now when you hear about royal houses with archangelic associations, or the Order of Melchizadek in the temples, you are hearing about events that took place in those enlightened kingdoms. The Order of Melchizadek in particular could only flourish in these kingdoms as it was very effective in its ability to hold and maintain large quantities of light. The blessings of this order in healing the populace and grounding light onto the planet played a large role in the few kingdoms in which they were present. The Order was forced to withdraw from the public eye during the Fourth Age.

The Order of Melchizadek grew from the days when the Archangel Melchizadek realised that the light was going from Atlantis. By initiating his priests himself he opened a conduit directly through to the centre of timeless space. This allowed the connection with the Creator of all, and the ability to hold the love of the Creator in person on Earth. How cut off you are, living as you do in a sealed universe, cut off from the love that created everything. This Order at the time of Atlantis was a rallying-point for all those who were unhappy with the central hierarchies. Because love and light were the foe of the prevailing evil, a core of resistance was maintained there. One of the other main functions of the Order of Melchizadek was that it was a repository of knowledge, the knowledge of the wider universe and stars, and knowledge of what life could be like. Inside the Order that which today looks like mysteries and magic was understood and used on a daily basis.

In these kingdoms of light the pattern of the warrior caste running society did not hold true. They were farmers, merchants and fisherman. Justice was upheld, not just the rule of law which is a burden to you now, but actual justice for all. The hereditary ruling family could hear and see their archangelic guides as advisors in running the kingdom. Those days reached a pinnacle for the Archangelic Collective to see what life and society could be like here when we were visible.

There were other kingdoms, many of which you might place in the middle, neither light nor dark also consisting of fishermen, farmers and merchants. In these the rulers always came from the warrior classes and were wholly supported by the lower classes. One of their members was the ruling king. In some this was hereditary, in others it changed frequently to the strongest member of the class. We had healing temples there as these were considered a good thing for the masses, as they would help the workers stay fit to pay their taxes. They were not frequented by the warriors themselves. They were not maintained and respected, and to be a healing priest there was to take your place on the margins of society. However there were always enough people to work in the temples, and they never ran short of priests.

The status of archangels and the attention paid to our advice varied through all these kingdoms. Sometimes we were listened to with care and the whole kingdom rose through the light and took its place with the few that were the most advanced from our perspective. Sometimes the opposite happened. There was still fluidity in the Atlantean society with countries rising and falling energetically from light to dark, as the coloured balls in one of those beautiful glass barometers.

In the final group of countries there was no place for us or our temples of healing. They were lands of slavery and darkness. All property there belonged to the king to hand out to those he found useful. Warriors were always well treated, and the general populace was worked to an early death to provide the upper echelons with luxuries. These countries preyed on their neighbours, which tended to be those of the middle type, for slaves and wealth. They produced very little themselves. The very worst of these was the kingdom of Gomorrah, whose name was remembered and included in your Bible's Old Testament in Genesis, along with that of the Order of Melchizadek.

What kind of place was Gomorrah? Your Bible tells the story of Lot, and the angel's search there for one good man to prevent its being destroyed (Genesis 19). This is a simplification of what happened, a teaching story. Before any such thing happened you had a black hole of a country that sucked into it the hapless stranger, other kingdoms, and the wealth of other countries. It tainted all that came into contact with it. It encouraged by example other countries to set up their societies in imitation of it, for there is always some unscrupulous and heartless person who can see personal benefit in lands filled with slaves. It was a disease spreading outwards. We watched this and tried to counsel moderation, but no one there would listen to us.

Gomorrah sank into darkness so deep that the waves of pain and suffering were etched into the surface of the planet. Many of the practices of human sacrifice and contempt for all humanity, and the belief that no other species had the right to exist began there. It was wholly evil and was responsible for a great deal of misery, and as we said, it was spreading to the surrounding kingdoms. The site of Gomorrah itself was the domain of demons, which were fat and happy on the energy produced there. This one country was an open door to allow blackness an entryway onto this planet and into humanity.

We did not act quickly enough to stem the flow of darkness. We had our client Kings and our healing temples and Orders where everything was going well. We thought we could protect them from being overwhelmed when the day of confrontation came. It never happened as a confrontation or battle, it happened as it always does, through first one, then another changing and influencing the general populace. Our beautiful kingdoms of light vanished in the end and were looted and destroyed by those who lived in them. There were very few remaining who could hear us or listened to our advice. When the last one perished the Fourth Age began.

Section Two

The Fourth Age

4

THE FOURTH AGE of Atlantis was the Age of Empires. The new empires ruled with harshness and cruelty, and the populations bled with the heavy burdens placed upon them.

New temples dominated the central cities where lines of captured slaves were burned in sacrificial fires to appease the "Gods". In this way the countryside was a source of food for the fires as well as food for the people; the temple fires burned twenty-four hours a day. Under the empires Atlantean society sank into a fog of fear and unhappiness for many generations.

Under the temples were the slave pits, and from there despair flowed out to the rest of the city. You can't imagine how this affected all of the people living there. It became harder and harder to remember what it was like to be joyful, to have simplicity in their lives, to be free to live happily and think loving thoughts. Fear was poisoning the lives of the city dwellers. The energy was so thick and dark they felt they were living in a dense fog, uncertain if they would be sent into the fires themselves. They became accustomed to living in fear and despair.

Those living in villages outside the cities were far enough away initially to resist the darkness, and continued to live with joy and love in their hearts. This is important because it led to a split that lasted until the very end of the continent. There were those who lived in the light as far from the centres as they could get, and there were the poor souls in the cities. Meanwhile villagers developed new ways of protecting themselves energetically, and new ways of defeating soldiers of the empires. The skirmishing and fighting never ended.

When the day came that waves rolled over the continent of Atlantis we could easily see who had light in their hearts. It is not something that can be hidden from higher beings. As we angels could see love, those who would destroy love could also see it and target those people. There was enough black energy generated by the temples of the Fourth Age to cause humanity to wander around in a haze, and forget what it was like to be human and free.

In addition to those burned in the temple fires, people were also seized for household slaves or as subjects in ongoing scientific experiments. Villagers made plans to safeguard the most precious knowledge so that it wouldn't be lost, and there was great sorrow as families were divided and prisoners taken away.

We wish to talk about those who were sold into the science experiments, as scientists had a stranglehold on Atlantis. They spoke with authority and were listened to by all sections of society. Their position was cemented into place on top of the hierarchy in the cities, and new experiments were discussed avidly throughout daily life, accepted without questioning. There was the promise of eternal life through cloning, and of newly manufactured slaves out of living body parts.

Cloning was only possible if the soul of the person being cloned was split, and the newly created half was used to bring the clone to life. This was not understood at the time. They made many such splits and clones for the wealthy, but at a terrible cost to the soul. As the soul shrank through division there was a loss of humanity. Life was animating the physical bodies, but the soul itself was fragmented. The cloned ceased to resist the ruler's demands for human sacrifices, or any other evil activity. Shallow and without moral strength, they were perfect vehicles to learn to be afraid of death, poverty, and change. These are the people who went down with Atlantis, and when they all died at once the souls recombined back into wholeness. We could see that this was necessary, but it was a hard way to perish. You are in danger of allowing cloning back into your world now and creating the same mistakes again.

Science in your days has been an active force for only the last few hundred years. In this period you will find most of the inventions and innovations that have cluttered up your lives. Before that time scientists were few and far between, and now you are educating as many as possible into this new religion. Why do we say religion? Because many scientific experiments are defended as being the 'truth' and the public is not allowed to challenge what is done in the lab. Many of your experiments are secret, and others are done only to prove that whoever is paying for the research is right. Not all research is sensibly devised, or done for the right reasons.

Your doctors design drug trials that may include a sugar pill for one of the trial groups. Often this group will also show improvement, and this is called the placebo effect. The placebo effect is accepted by the medical profession but not really respected by doctors, and because this is dismissed it is not fully understood. What helps is the patient's expectation of being healed and it has little to do with the doctor at all. Now look at other healing modalities from any culture around the world; only the patient's belief in healing matters. All other practices are just to help foster that belief. Everyone heals themselves, and they are the only ones who can.

Among the plans hidden by the coastal villagers were energetic blueprints for a healthy world, a world that was made only of love and joy. These plans are still in existence today, but it is not the right time yet to unfold them across the planet. That day will come. Other plans involved resistance groups, and importantly these are the groups that did not go under when Atlantis foundered. These people lived near the coasts and had access to ships, and when the land began to shake and everyone who was able embarked, they found monsters of the deep waiting for them. We did our best to get people past the monsters with the fewest losses.

Where did they land? For the most part they landed in the British Isles, Ireland and Europe, with many others founding ancient Egypt and long-forgotten African civilisations. A few went to the West and landed in the Americas also. The effect of these good servants of the light landing in these countries changed the neighbouring civilisations by anchoring the light in these areas. In Britain and Egypt the knowledge remained to construct some mighty works such as the stone circles at Avebury and the pyramids.

The early British societies were Atlantean, and we consider Arthur the last Atlantean king of these Isles. He predates recorded history because he has been hidden in the Time of Legends, and we would like to talk some more about him in the final section of this book. The stone circles at Avebury with Silbury Hill as its counterpart are Atlantean technology, and they are being readied by those who work for the light to resume their purpose when the time is right. Very soon, when they are ready to be activated, the Earth as you know it will change.

5

DURING THE Fourth Age in Atlantis we angels could not influence the overwhelming majority who were living in fear, as if fear was all there was to life. They moved through their days with a heaviness sending them ever deeper into misery. Joy is love, love is light, and there is no love without joy. Many of these people resembled zombies to us, hollow shells with their humanity tucked down so deep inside it was no longer the controlling force. You can still spot people like this today if you look closely, and the Atlanteans were being ruled by such as these. Our role as guides was impossible; we were being shut out by the concentration of unhappiness in the cities and by those who benefited from the overall misery. We were only able to affect the villages nearest the sea, furthest away from the cities. Even there the people had stopped seeing us, believing there was no one to see.

The ordinary citizens of the day were coerced into keeping quiet and attending the temples to watch as the prisoners died. They came away from those ceremonies literally drained of energy as their fear was part of the dark energy produced at these events. Citizens thought life in the cities was normal because they knew no other way to live. In the marketplaces people would hide and cower as the soldiers marched by on raiding parties, taking whatever they desired.

The lower classes, all those who were not in the top echelons of the hierarchy, were free people and citizens but their lives were at the disposal of the rulers. This was a frightening time to be alive. The food for the cities was grown by the people, but in the fields surrounding the cities the crops began to fail as the Earth drew back her energy from all that was happening. She shut down the parts that were closest to the damage so as to avoid feeling the pain of those areas, and it was like trying to grow crops in lifeless soil. The lack of food sent raiding parties further afield to take what was required. There would be clashes as the armies of different empires met one another in the central farmlands, and there were frequent raids. In the outlying farms and villages they lived with the uncertainty of warfare for generations.

There was no peace either in the coastal villages where the raiding parties captured slaves and prisoners. In those villages the old ways had continued and the Earth was honoured, and love and respect were shown to everyone. The people respected the Earth, and they continued the Reiki circles from the earlier Atlantean periods. In your day it is the tribes that live closest in nature to the Earth that have maintained their care for the planet itself. The coastal villages were targeted for these reasons, as they were the centres for light.

In the cities it seemed like society and normal life were happening. There were dinner parties and other social get-togethers, newspapers, music, books and theatre. Their houses were warmed by the crystal energy as a gift from the Earth, and they had running water and other necessary conveniences. Some of you would feel very at home there, and marvel at their standard of living, their servants, and their elegance, but it was like a scab over a dirty wound.

At the top of the hierarchy was the Emperor with his court, the army and the scientists living in great wealth. They were misled, believing the promptings of their empty hearts and refused to give up their wealth and position and die at the end of their natural lifetimes. To them, having others die so they might live was acceptable.

6

HOW COULD life be prolonged? So began the science experiments. Better yet, could life be immortal? Initially they devised medicines and concoctions to prolong their lives. By the Fourth Age they could expect to live about ninety years, down from hundreds of years in the earlier ages before they split into male and female. They felt very vulnerable to death. As time went by they advanced their surgery to incorporate organ and limb transplants from "donors", usually those scheduled for sacrifices. It made old age more comfortable, but did not prolong their lives and they gave up their bodies ever more reluctantly. In the end they developed their cloning techniques.

Cloning began when people became reluctant and resentful about dying. There were many in the upper classes who felt that scientists should be able to find a way of prolonging their lives. This led to an interesting period where scientists had all the money they needed to study how to increase life spans and reverse aging. Everyone felt they had a common interest in these experiments and discussed them continually. Initially the experiments revolved around replacing worn out body parts from donors, originally those condemned to die. They tried growing spare parts in vats made out of stem cells. While these partial solutions did not lead to longer lives, they coarsened those who did this research and they lost their sense of right and wrong. Later they developed cloning as the only way to keep a soul continuously in a body on Earth. Many, many died while this was being developed, most often prisoners.

Cloning involved a tremendous amount of energy to split the body and soul and reproduce another version of themselves. The client would enter a machine and undergo the division. Choices were available, and he or she would be the new clone, but much younger. The brain would be duplicated inside two heads, and the age of the clone would be chosen before starting the process. At the end he could look into his own eyes looking back at him.

The clone would be taken home to live; the original anticipating a continuation of life when the old body died. The new clone was looked after and fed, but not expected to live a fulfilling life until the original was dead. That was in the beginning, but problems soon began to develop. The soul was split now, and there was a dramatic change in personality. Friends became unrecognizable, ruthless and hard. Some clones were raised for body parts for the original client, and a living being with a soul was dismembered and killed for replacement organs and limbs without consideration or understanding.

Atlanteans had forgotten that souls would reincarnate over and over again, remembering only that the soul went on elsewhere after the body died. Because they believed they only had one life to live they thought they could achieve immortality by moving their soul into a new body. The purpose of having many different lives was forgotten.

They did not understand that to create a clone was to rip away part of their own soul, thinking the clones were simply a replica of their own body and would only be complete when their soul took possession. They failed to comprehend that the being animating their clone in the meantime was themselves, and not just a type of robotic temporary space saver that was part of the scientific process. Clones were believed to be spare bodies that were not complete human beings with human desires and human thoughts and emotions. It would not be a real human being until the original soul that created it had passed over into it from its own dying body.

When the original human being was at the point of death, a clone would be brought into their room and the 'temporary' personality inside told to step aside so that the 'real' soul of the dying person could take over. Immortality was attained with ever renewable bodies.

When asked to vacate their soul a clone usually did, because they had been conditioned to do so throughout their entire existence. Occasionally they refused completely and were killed as having no further purpose, or refused secretly and pretended to be the original after his death.

The clone's soul would not return to the higher dimensions to wait and consider the life that had just ended. It remained attached to all other living clones of the same soul by energetic lines, a little like a spider's web. It was a ghost, denied the chance to learn from its life. Some people had a quite a few clones, one or more for body parts, one as a replacement if he should die, one as a little baby to grow up with himself as guardian. The more the soul was split, the less soul there was to inhabit each body. These bodies were easy to hijack by dark entities that lived off their physical energy.

Your soul at this time is intact, and some of you have been incarnating for many lifetimes. Your purpose in having so many incarnations is to learn about who you are as a member of the universal family of light. By dividing your soul from your bodies (which is ordinarily how you would see death), then parcelling it out to other bodies as clones you entered a world of exhaustion and delusion. Your individual souls were never intended to animate more than one body at a time. The fact that there were overlapping incarnations meant the soul's learning process had stagnated and ground to a halt. The purpose of cloning was to continue living one life in a position of wealth and property forever.

You have learned many things by having many different experiences, and its how your game was set up to be played in the distant past. When we talk about taking a human soul and dividing it into pieces you do not know what that would feel like. This is where you will have to trust us about what we observed in Atlantis; that a soul divided is a soul that no longer can feel love. We care about whether or not you have love present in your souls, as love is light. We are angels of light and we strive to spread light across the universe and across this planet. When these souls divided and lost the ability to love it was another way to spread fear and darkness. For us, cloning was a new device to cancel the light and we did not like this development at all.

In the beginning there was the great human soul, the unifying force of humanity. It divided into people and seems to be capable of infinitely dividing into humans as your population soared. You each have a soul present in your bodies today. When the soul leaves your body you know the body has died for this lifetime and the soul has returned to the higher dimensions to make plans for the next incarnation. These new splintered souls, where the person's soul was continually present on Earth meant they did not learn from a variety of new experiences or make any new plans. If you thought that you might be the one who was to be a human sacrifice in your next life, would you be quite so quick about putting others in the flames? This is exactly the type of lesson that you like to arrange for yourselves, seeing life from every angle so that you learn everything you can.

Those who could afford a series of clones did not leave the planet or reincarnate to have a multitude of experiences.

Doesn't this sound like a great deal for the wealthy? Why have lives of poverty if you could live forever in luxury? The individuals concerned paid a very high price for this. They were like zombies, and those who did not have enough of a soul left to keep out the darkness became puppets of dark entities and lived their lives generating and living off fear. This was the reality of the upper classes, rulers, scientists and army officers alike. The cities were run by dark entities masquerading as humans and they were very happy to facilitate the human sacrifices, as they had little humanity left to them.

As time went by we watched with horror as the younger clones did not wait for the older ones to die before grabbing their share of the power, and murdered their owners. We no longer saw any value to this society tearing itself apart. We thought we were looking at another lost cause; that humanity was not going to come out of this game but be stuck in the unhappiness forever.

We were sorry for the human soul and the path it was taking, but we would have left your situation alone except for one thing, the Earth itself asked us for help. Our hearts went out to her and we worked out our plan to help by removing the continent completely from her surface. The waves crashed in and only a few of the people escaped in boats to found new societies on other continents. The clones all died at once and reunited in the higher dimensions where they were able to take stock of what had happened below. The reunited souls were relieved to reassemble and continue to learn in the way set out by your larger soul group. They had learned one thing, that an intact soul is priceless.

7

WHAT DISTURBED us most was humanity being tricked into laying aside their morals within their society. The cloning experiments did not arise out of an outside group: they were sought after and funded by the people of Atlantis. The funding was arranged by the state for the greater good of all the people, but none save the wealthiest could afford cloning. It elevated scientists from a position of service to the populace to well-paid celebrities who began to practice their skills only for money. They lost the ability to see Atlanteans as people with families who were missing them, who loved and were loved; these human subjects became science experiments. Once cloning was successful, all scientists were cloned for the good of the state.

Cloning was the beginning of the end for Atlantis, more for the clone's hardness of heart than for science itself. Humans had a goal when they began their time here on Earth, and it involved learning about themselves as a soul group, and that soul group's relationship to the Creator. This learning continued after death, and before the next life. It was hard to remember this when alive and busy living, but humanity was making progress in a slow fashion. Cloning not only stopped all learning, it stagnated into cruelty. Cruel things still happen in your world today and shock you, but this was a cruel society; no one seemed to feel shock anymore or recognize themselves in other living people. You are all one soul and nothing small, like the colour of your eyes, can divide you.

Now let us return to when the dark days of Atlantis were in full flow, not to be reversed until the continent was removed. The slaving parties continued so there would always be someone to feed to the fires and the coastal villages never got the chance to grow in size. One by one those villages were being wiped out completely, and those who could not be captured were left behind dead. There was knowledge in these villages to maintain health and well-being, and knowledge too of how to fight back. Some of this knowledge was not completely lost and is still here today.

The villagers began to plan for a future where there was light after the darkness. We helped them hide their plans so that they would remain hidden until the day when it was safe for them to be activated. When the day comes, there are plans to reverse much of the damage to the Earth, and to humanity. The plans will unfold and what is hidden in them will come forth.

One of the main activities in the villages was boat building. Coastal villages were fishing as well as farming communities, and they started to build larger boats to find somewhere else to live besides the green land of Atlantis. These villages started to explore the surrounding continents, and did not always return safely. Therefore the boats were ready and built when the island was removed and the waves rolled over. Many of the villages evacuated completely at that time and rode to safety on the waves. They scattered in many different directions and settled intact in clans and family groups on other continents. Because they stayed together they were able to bring with them some of the useful values and knowledge that had been part of their lives.

Just before the end in Atlantis, there was fighting between those who had ruled for millennia and those who lived and worked in the lower classes. The hierarchy competed among themselves to see who could amass the greatest wealth and keep it by never dying. Those outside the ruling classes grouped together in the cities and murdered and took what they felt they had a right to. There were clashes of armed groups in the streets and loyalties swapped back and forth to the highest bidder, and many who were innocent died at this time. Life became very uncertain for all.

This was a time of chaos and desperation. The very wealthy were safe behind their walls and private armies. However they were no longer safe from their own clones. Even if their younger clones were kept away from the main residence they were the same callous person inside another body. More and more frequently they chose to murder the original and assume his powerful position. Clones were able to do this by commanding loyalty among the servants, who chose to support the younger man, the future employer. When the younger man took the original's place these people were rewarded. How long did this go on? You must imagine generations, with each subsequent generation less human than the one before. The amount of soul available to divide was not as great as at the original cloning. Wealth and power were concentrated in the hands of the semi-human.

There is more than one way to be less than human. Some of you today look at others and say there is something physical about them that make them less than human. When we look at you and your temporary bodies we seldom focus on what your body is like, we look at your soul. Some of you have very bright souls carrying love and understanding. Some souls have a long way to go, and some have been deprived for lifetimes of the ability to run your own lives. Sometimes there is a dark entity that attaches to a soul and lives the life as its own for lifetime after lifetime living off the energy of the person. Because being incarnate is where the opportunity is for learning this is a serious deprivation and interference. We would encourage you to seek help in all such cases. Ask us, the angels of light, for help and we will help you. Your soul is immortal and you need never fear the death of your current body.

At the end skirmishing and civil war reached from the countryside into the cities themselves. If Atlantis had carried on in this way we felt that the population would have destroyed itself. The civilisation was being torn apart.

Section Three

The End of
the Fourth Age

8

THERE WERE many uses of cloning in Atlantis. Farm animals were cloned almost as a matter of course at the end. It did not matter that their cloned lives were shorter than the originals to the owners, as their lives had been shortened by farming practices anyway. The animals suffered from this in exactly the same way that the human clones suffered. Animals are not put here just to be food for humans; they all have their own objectives in living as well as a communal soul. They have varied and complicated lives, and the right to get on with their births and deaths as planned. Cloning was reproducing a human-desired specimen over and over again, without regard to what is natural. Cloning removed an animal from the natural order and made it something unnatural as far as its soul was concerned. Now that you have cloned farm animals in your laboratories again, we see that you still do not know what a soul is or the harm you can do to it.

One of the much discussed experiments of the time was the creation of new slaves by combining animal parts with human body parts. Everyone had a view on what would make the best slave. It is possible to slice up living organisms and combine them using lasers; the technology is being used again today on viruses. These poor creatures would wake up and find they had a dismembered soul, and be made to work in industry and on farms. The scientists tried over and over again to attach animal parts to human slaves, but often these beings would die, although every now and then one would live. They never understood that the soul of the human could not absorb the partial souls of the combined animals, nor could it ignore them either. There is a little talk now about heart transplants influencing the recipient's personality, but it is more a case of the new heart muscle having a memory of the donor's soul, rather than actually containing a sliver of it. In Atlantis these multi-soul combinations were confused beings, neither one thing nor another. They were able to live by giving up the control of the new being to an entity that could plug in and use the life form. Not ideal by any means, but it was easy for an entity to gain control and it worked as an energy source for them.

There was such an element of cruelty to these experiments, such hardness of heart that would cut still-living limbs from animals and weld them together or onto a human to increase his number of arms or give him an appendage that would help in multi-tasking. This culture no longer incorporated love or respect for others or the Earth. There has never been a time since as bad as the Fourth Age of Atlantis. We were helpless to intervene, and could only watch as this civilisation slid into darkness.

When the experiments against the crystals began, just to see if they could be turned from light to dark, the Earth and the crystals asked us to intervene. We consulted how we could best help, and in the end we lifted the continent of Atlantis out of the physical realms of the Earth. When we raised it into the higher dimensions it vanished from sight for humanity, but it remained a problem for the Earth. It was like cutting out a major organ and leaving it still connected an arm's length from your body. It impeded the flow of energy around the Earth and she was never as well and healthy from that point onwards. Also there was a great wrenching and tearing through her energy fields and in the higher dimensions. Some of the Earth's elementals (higher dimensional beings such as dragons, elves, etc.) were trapped for many ages in the damage that was done then. Much work has been done by some humans recently to release these and there have been improvements.

The Mook were minstrel elementals of that time that travelled seasonally throughout the dimensions. They were travellers as well as musicians, and their travels through the twelve dimensions allowed them to mix the dimensions as a spoon mixes in a bowl. On the day that Atlantis was wrenched away most of these were trapped in the rifts that were made in the energy systems of the Earth. They were caught and frozen in place, with arms and legs in different dimensions from each other. Not only did their music become silent, but their role as mixers of the dimensions ended. The dimensions became stagnant, and separated into layers with little movement between them. It is only recently they have been freed by humans from the rift, their arms and legs disentangled, and the dimensions have regained some of their flow.

We angels are all about flow and light, and the Mook were elementals of light that had a role to play in the health of the Earth. The many years of stagnation did not benefit the Earth or us. Now the Mook are mixing and stirring the dimensions it is easier for us to come to you and speak with you again. There have not been such opportunities for communication and guidance in all the years since Atlantis fell, and for those who can hear there is now once again music of joy on the Earth. The Mook are being used here as an example of how things can go awry as side effects of larger problems, and because they are in higher dimensions you are not aware of all that has gone wrong around you as a result of the downfall.

9

WHEN THE Mook were frozen at the ruin of Atlantis, there were other catastrophes that took place with the non-humans. There were crystal deaths at that time, whose lives were snuffed out before the island was ever destroyed. The crystals accepted energy from the Earth itself and passed it on to humans for their needs, such as warming their houses and providing light and power. When energy was needed for the cloning experiments they had all the power they needed. Near the end of Atlantis there were experiments to see what it would take to either kill the crystals or reverse the flow. The objective was malign; if a way could be found to reverse the flow through the crystals, then the Earth herself would be poisoned.

Crystals at that time were fairly stationary but sentient, and seemed easy prey. If the Atlanteans would not hesitate to harm another living being, why not harm the crystals and the planet? This is incomprehensible to us, quite honestly. Why harm the planet you live on? Do you think you'll get another one easily? Today again you do not trouble yourselves to care for her. Learn from your past mistakes and return love and respect to the planet that gives you a place to live!

When dark energy is pushed through a crystal of light it will kill it. The crystals reached enlightenment when they were the dominant life force on this planet and they remained behind to help the Earth and the other races that came here to live. When some of these crystals were under attack it was a little like slicing off a human's toes. Not pleasant, but not fatal except for the toes. These poor crystals were left alone to die, cut off from the crystal consciousness to protect it from dying through them. In their many lifetimes of service the crystals did nothing to merit this unjust attack. Now the crystals joined the Earth to plead with us for their lives, to remove Atlantis before there were any more deaths.

We went back to the One who is both light and dark, and we formulated our plans for rescue. The most appropriate angels and beings of light returned with us to lift the archipelago out of the ocean and allow the human bodies to die. Only those who lived by the light along the edges of the continent escaped in their boats, and there were no survivors at all from the cities. There were no kingdoms of 'dark Atlanteans' that survived anywhere.

This scattering of the coastal peoples came in time to save them from total annihilation by the Atlanteans who lived in the cities. It allowed a smaller population to assimilate into the villages where they landed, and teach them. Many human souls repaired themselves in the higher dimensions, and this was the most important element to us. The cloned souls were a dead end for humanity, and all the souls came home at once and recombined. They became whole again. When they next incarnated they were at full capacity, they could love and live with all the gifts of being human. This was one good outcome from such a violent act.

The souls who were never cloned and who were agents of light, learned more over the generations of the Fourth Age by reincarnating and living, than the ones who lived long, ongoing cloned lifetimes that were virtually the same. These cloned souls were behind in learning about what it is to be fully human. In your world today many of the advanced Atlantean souls are here again now and working for the angels of light. They are here because it is time for change, and you are putting forward your best people. Atlantis vanished, but some of her ideas have been resurfacing lately, and not the good ones. There will not be any room for clones again in the Earth of the future; or the lack of kindness that made slaves out of beings made of combined body parts. Those of you who have come a long way will be able to help the others, and there is only one great human soul. It stays together as one whole soul no matter how many times it is fragmented, and that is the only option open. There are no sub-humans, you are all the same. Remember all other human beings carry a tiny part of you inside themselves.

The day came when our plans were ready and we removed Atlantis from the physical surface of the Earth. Together we watched the destruction that resulted from our unified actions and we placed the higher dimensional continent into the energy fields of the Earth. We watched the almost complete annihilation of the Atlanteans. Very few survived.

Boats washed up in many different locations and people carried the advanced Atlantean knowledge with them. England and France erected their stone circles in the most suitable places, and people were taught about the planet and how they could help stabilise her. For many centuries the main focus of the new civilisations around the edges of the Atlantic Ocean was to help stabilise the Earth, who had undergone a terrible, almost unimaginable shock. The Earth's partnership with humanity was resumed.

Some areas were storehouses of Atlantean knowledge. This was deliberate so that not everything would be lost, and some of the good and hard-won advances would be available for the human race. Now we come to a difference in what you would see as advances and what we would see as advances. Pyramids are a good example of physical advances by humanity where natural law is used to create giant structures of stone. We value instead the advances people made toward caring for the Earth, and grounding and holding light. The largest reservoirs of light ever made on this planet are the pyramids, and yet that is not how you see them at all. Priests and priestesses daily filled these structures with the love and light of the universe so the people would live in a fertile land. Ancient Egypt was a blessed realm, and much that was known there could still be discovered by you today. Nothing is more important than to learn to fill yourselves with light through Reiki or another similar healing system.

Although ancient Egypt existed for many years as a stable Atlantean monarchy, this was not the case everywhere. Because Egypt was stable there were many Atlantean skills in use there for a very long time. You marvel at the pyramids that were made using very ordinary skills and an understanding of natural laws, and how to use these laws to levitate stone.

Egypt is a subject that could fill a book by itself.

10

THE END OF Atlantis came very swiftly after much planning on our part. The intent was to scatter the survivor's boats widely, as we felt that the intermingling of the Atlanteans with the people who had fallen behind in culture on the surrounding continents would be beneficial. It was not just that others could learn from Atlanteans, but that knowledge could be exchanged. Living in fear had atrophied some of the emotions and qualities that we knew humanity needed.

The villages on the African coasts had an understanding of joy and how to live with others joyfully. Joy is a particularly beloved kind of light and strands of joy were part of the lives of the natives of these villages. We wish everyone alive could learn this much about joy from people who really know about it and maintain it in their lives in the face of everything. Joy is not being simplistic; it is being in touch with the universe. Together they formed great and sophisticated civilisations that vanished a long time ago.

The Celtic people were blessed with music to set the emotions flowing and free. Their music had liveliness which has been maintained in the face of the popular dirges called hymns for many centuries. In Atlantis we used music in our temples to bring emotional release. This was twofold as health results when emotions are not bottled up, and releasing happy emotions allows them to be shared. Did you ever think that joy is something to be built up and released so it flows across the land? When you think of dancing to Irish fiddle music does it make you smile? Why was something that gave so much joy ever treated as second class? The very tones of music are healing, either to be immersed in or through creating them, or just by being present when music is played. 'New age' music is not always healing and we caution you to assess how you feel when you hear this music being played. It is not possible for you to step into someone else's life and listen to music through their ears; also someone else's choice in music is not to be judged by you.

The descendents of the Celts now live on the Atlantic coastal fringes of Ireland, Scotland, Scandinavia, France, and Spain. They lived in the deep past and roamed all over Europe, and had quite different lives to anything you might expect now. They lived on a planet that was still fully connected to the rest of the universe and part of their lives were spent in maintaining that open connection. They ran under the stars and their feet beat the universal rhythm of the spheres, the same beat as the beat of the Earth's heart, the rhythm of life. At these times they maintained their collective consciousness and resembled flocks of birds more than humans in their ability to turn and run as one under the trees. The faster they ran and the faster the beat sped up into one tone the closer they came to the universe and each other. The final period of running was the ecstasy of connection to the Source and the Earth, it allowed no impediments to the flow of light and energy. Sometimes you can feel the speed and excitement build during an Irish or Scottish ceilidh dance.

The rhythm of the Source is the heartbeat of the universe. As it flows outward from the centre we feel the impulse of love from the heart of the Creator, and as it flows inwards the Creator receives it back from us in a two-way flow and exchange. It is a perfect example of the microcosm being a reflection of the macrocosm, where the human circulatory system works exactly the same as the universe as a whole. Our hearts pump new life and energy around the body, and new life and energy is pumped from the Source and the experiences of life are pumped back. It is a closed system. However this planet has long been out of touch with these energies and makes do with the most minimal flow imaginable. If part of your body were this restricted it would be dying.

Long ago on the coasts of Europe the Celts welcomed the Atlanteans as teachers and learned to see with their eyes. There was an exchange, for the Atlanteans had developed their Reiki circles because they lived on a pastoral and agricultural island. The Celts had benefited from living under the endless trees in the vast forests of Europe. The trees on this planet have acted as the guardians of the humans from the beginning. They enabled life with their carbon dioxide exchange, shelter and nuts, they taught the humans through their wisdom. The genetic pool of Atlanteans had grown distinct over the years spent in isolation, and there was interbreeding when they landed. There have been no true Celts now for many, many years.

North America was home to people who understood how to live with the Earth as you know how to live with your next door neighbours. She was honoured by them and lived with them. Again this was a society who danced on the ground, whose feet beat the rhythm of life. Those of you who live in North America do not know what the Earth can be like when she is not withdrawn and shut down, but connected. Of all the places in the world, the continent that was the most alive the longest is now the most shut down. The Native Americans maintained the health of the land instinctively through their feet and their living practices. They understood that the Earth was one being and they were another, and there could be no ownership in their relationship. There was companionship between the Earth and those who lived there until recently.

Some of the beneficial practices of the Native Americans are studied today by people who wish to come closer to the Earth. These practices contain within them the seeds of healthy living for all parties. Respect and balance, joy and fun were all part of their lives. Sometimes they did not live this way, but practiced genocide against other tribes. We have seen this pattern happen among humans so many times on this planet that we would not want to see anyone held up as the perfect example of how to live. In the end you will be perfect in time for ascension, before then you are still learning everything the hard way.

Another place Atlanteans landed was Central and South America. In that area they were able to make their own villages and resume their lives based on Atlantean fishing and farming. This area was empty before they arrived. Although they had no one to teach on their arrival, for many generations they led fruitful Atlantean-style lives. Even there, where they built their large cities in imitation of Atlantis, they were not able to maintain their connection to the universe or the light.

Much is talked about the missing population and wisdom of the Mayan people who settled so far in the distant past that it is difficult to relate your discovered ruins with that civilisation. Mayan civilisation peaked millennia ago after they spread across the Central and South American land masses. In the beginning they continued their Atlantean ways and honoured the Earth. They built their stone temples and cities and farmed in the Atlantean manner. This was the seed of their destruction in the end; it is very hard to maintain farming and hard manual work as the basis of any civilisation. There is not enough joyful living in hard work.

They were educated in the ways of the universe beyond today's comprehension, and they carried into their society our teachings from generations past.

The Mayans existed for a long, long time but in the end they disintegrated as a society and vanished. Some of these people turned into the hunter-gathers of the Amazon basin and resumed a life that is primitive and brief, but contain elements of joy and stepping lightly upon the Earth. Others are long gone and their influence is forgotten. The Mayan calendar that shows the current cycle of the world ending in 2012 is the one piece of ancient wisdom that we wished to pass on to you. We protected it and made sure that you received it today. This calendar shows the end of a great stellar cycle of the rhythm and flow of energy across the universe. It was set in motion a long time ago as a wave of energy due to arrive here in 2012. This is not something to take personally as meant for the human race, but as an event that touches all planets, moons and stars as it rolls past in waves. It will affect all life as it washes past and cleanses with love. This date was preserved for you so you could prepare yourselves. (Preparation covered in Planet Earth Today.)

The final place where a number of ships landed was north in the snow covered lands. Vast cities were built underground below the snow and ice. These cities are still there but you do not know of them. They will not open to you until the very end of your time on the surface, when you all become one again. These cities have a different history and practices, and we will not be talking further of them now. There is much of interest to archaeologists buried under the ice of Northern Canada and Greenland that will change the way you look at your own history and dates.

The survivors of Atlantis were not the priests and priestesses of the inner temples, but the ordinary people.

The leaders that came with them were the local wise men and healers, and even their wisdom was enough to heal and keep the people and the Earth happy. When they met and intermingled with the humans on the other continents they seemed like Gods. Their Atlantean knowledge taught and nurtured by angels was far above that of the local people. But during their time in Atlantis they had lost something of joy and love and it was this other people remembered and were able to teach them. Sometimes even out of the worst catastrophes some good may come.

11

IN THE EARLY days the shipwrecked Atlanteans formed two major civilisations on the planet, one each in the northern and southern hemispheres. This was at a time when there was no ice on Antarctica, and the vast southern civilisation existed in a ring around present day South America, Antarctica, and Africa. What was this civilisation like? The temples were gone, and suddenly the people were blended with others in a seemingly limitless landscape. They now had space and land of varying terrain for growing food, where before they had a blessed island realm. There were large cities built on these continents that are now beneath the waves of the Atlantic, where no traces will ever be found of them. These were high societies of skill, wealth and knowledge, all run by enlightened rulers who had no wish to repeat the mistakes of the past.

The Southern civilisation existed for thousands of years, for the most part benevolently. They returned to seafaring, fishing, and farming; they used science wisely and kept their populations balanced with the amount of food and land available. Space was left for animals and other inhabitants to live, and for the Earth herself to have a volcano or earthquake. In this way equilibrium was maintained for a long, long time.

The Northern civilisation circled around North Africa, Europe, Greenland, and North America. They had a slightly different history, less sunny and more intense, they remained on a war footing much of the time. They were strong and beautiful, and lived with the trees and animals in closer harmony. They had sophisticated cities and knowledge like the southern civilisation, but adapted to their climate and landscape. The great difference was that another civilisation was pushing at them from the East, from the direction of Asia today. Because of this they had a tougher edge, and worked harder to protect their culture. These were the people who put up the first stone circles in Europe. The circles shifted position over time as required.

The great Southern civilisation gradually broke apart into sections, but not until they had sent out many colonies around the world. Only the aboriginals of Australia retain a small part of the knowledge from that time. They remember the land as part of their family and how to live with her. When other less important things were forgotten they hung onto the knowledge that matters.

The Northern civilisation drew its strength from the ground it lived on, and from the natural life it was surrounded with. The cities contained as much knowledge and sophistication as the Southern Atlantean cities but they felt different; there were fewer fields among the trees and the houses were made from wood which gleamed when polished. Because the houses were made of wood there was a closer relationship with the living trees. The relationship with trees that live for years is deeper than the relationship with an annual crop, and the trees were seen as part of their communities. Trees remember and share a consciousness, they communicate with other plants and animals and the Earth itself through their roots. The news of the advancing army of the Eastern civilisation would come almost instantaneously through the trees to the people.

This Eastern civilisation was a warlike one that had developed over the millennia the Atlanteans lived on their islands. It did not have the scientific learning of Atlantis, nor had as much of our angelic teaching over their years of development, but neither did it have the depths of cruelty or inhumanity. We had also been present there, but had not been able to make a consistent impact on them. We were dealing with a very diverse population of small separate groups while the Atlanteans were one group at their beginning. The separate groups were very unlike one another in the way they lived, some were warlike raiders, others were peaceful farmers. They had different expectations of what constituted a whole life. In the end they were gathered together as a confederacy under the kingship of the strongest of the warlike tribes, not for the purpose of living together in cities, but to raid and take slaves from others. It seemed better to be part of the group than be attacked by them. They constantly pushed at the edges of the Northern Atlantean civilisation.

It is a long time ago now that this movement of tribes came from the East, and it has rarely stopped since then. Even your recent European history records invaders from the East. They were drawn westwards in wonder, and to have the land and cities for themselves. The wealth of the civilisations that were established post-Atlantis was something they wanted to possess. When they battered at the outer edges of the civilisation they felt they could live the same way the Atlanteans lived. This was one of those moments that may have changed everything that came later, because instead of the Atlanteans teaching them about the ancient wisdoms they shut them out and spent their strength and wealth in battle. They had become arrogant and did not want to teach new people to be the same as they were and would not include them. They did not see that they were all one human soul.

It would have been better had the Atlanteans welcomed the newcomers into their cities and taught them to care for the Earth, and helped them learn who they were as human beings. These Eastern kingdoms emerged again and again as the enemy, fighting for what would not be shared or given; and they were treated as different or lesser beings. In the end they fought against King Arthur at Glastonbury with cold determination. That war saw the final weakening and end of the post-Atlantean civilisations. Life continued, but people no longer remembered their purpose in being alive. There had been long years of contentment in the early Atlantean ages when people knew why they were alive, and this was still part of the later civilisations. When it was forgotten the foundation of their societies became unstable, and the search for the meaning of life began all over again.

We spoke in detail in *Planet Earth Today* about the need for the Creator to learn about himself by experiencing life, and everything in the universe exists to provide these experiences. This is the purpose of your lives here.

The effect of the post-Atlanteans' decision not to share their knowledge with outsiders led to the decline of a great civilisation. As in the Fourth Age, people forgot who they were and why they were on Earth. They forgot to care for the Earth and keep their side of the contract with her. Their lives lost direction and their actions became harmful to other life forms and the planet itself. This is where you find yourself today, and why we are writing books to remind you of your long history. We want you to remember who you are as one of the souls of light in this universe, with a plan and a purpose. You have time, just, to remember and begin to live your lives with knowledge and understanding of your reason for being here. We know you will be able to do this.

12

THE NORTHERN Atlanteans used many valuable resources to defend and protect their cities, and in the movement of people from place to place there was a break in the transfer of knowledge between the generations. The cities contained their vibrancy and shared knowledge far longer where they kept records in writing. With oral information it only takes one person to forget to teach another and it's lost forever. Information vanished about living with the Earth, the truths of the universe, and the history of the human race and its role as an incarnate soul. Why are we here? It is a question to which every child once knew the answer. How do we live whole and complete lives? What are the stars? And so forth.

After a while both of the great civilisations forgot why they built pyramids (for example) and continued to build them because they had always been built. The new pyramids were not quite as large as the old Atlantean ones, and they didn't work in the same way, but they kept building them. (Atlantean pyramids were built to focus a powerful incoming stream of universal energy and disperse it widely into the ground, for the Earth's use. Pyramids built by Egyptians, Canary Islanders, Central Americans, etc. were far less effective.) Many things are done now, and were done then, without an understanding of why they are done. Reasons are manufactured to explain a practice when the truth has been forgotten. The only people who still remember why they do some of the things they do are the Australian aborigines. The people who have forgotten the most are the "western" civilisations that everyone is so eager to copy. When something is done without understanding why it is done, it has no meaning.

The effect was to diminish this great civilisation more quickly, and there was an early fragmentation into smaller kingdoms, and they became less sophisticated as time went by. In the end there were two kingdoms that remained with the most Atlantean knowledge; one was Egypt where the history you are familiar with is the rustic end of a great and long Atlantean civilisation. The other was Britain, blessed by the energy of the great stone circles they maintained. These stone circles provided protection and stability for many years until their purpose was forgotten and they were left to decay. They truly function now only in the higher dimensions.

Britain is the part of the Earth containing the engine, drawing in the universal energy and using it like the human body uses its heart. The light is pumped around the energy lines in the depths of the Earth and near the surface. If your body did not have blood pumped around it would stagnate and die, and the Earth has been in the position of a heart attack patient waiting for her heart to be restarted by paramedics. She doesn't die in minutes the way you would, but she's been waiting for help for centuries. When the engine was restarted in 2010 she was running down towards death.

At the time of the North Atlantic civilisation Britain was the centre of learning, where the more advanced skills and knowledge to keep the Earth functioning healthily were in daily use. Generations were trained in the maintenance of the stone circles, monitoring the flows of energy from the stars and moving the circles to the right places. People would come from other countries to learn how to keep their land healthy and where to place their own stone circles. In some ways this was an improvement from the days when only Atlanteans looked after the Earth. What could be more important than keeping the land healthy, when the land looked after those who lived on it? The greatest understanding of the planet at that time was in Britain. Later Egypt used other methods to keep the Earth healthy.

Because Britain had the site of Avebury to maintain (the stones have been replaced there time and again) it became a very cosmopolitan country. Those who wished to work with the Earth and learn from the universal energy would make long visits there. It was understood that the energy itself was the teacher and healer in many cases, and those who were ill knew how to rebalance themselves in the great circle. As long as they kept the circle of Avebury maintained and protected, in Britain the light shone the brightest.

After the final battle where King Arthur died, humanity was left with a vacuum of knowledge. The teachers who knew about the Earth simply were no longer there, and the remaining people were left with stone circles to maintain. They knew these were important and maintained them over millennia as features of the landscape without understanding why. The old teachers knew when a stone was ready to be moved and their work was practical, not ceremonial. The students who survived had no idea how to tell when and neglected that part of their work. Instead they developed rituals and ceremonies to take the place of actual work.

Avebury and Stonehenge became great centres of ceremony with other nearby henges such as Woodhenge. People participated and felt better by being there but it was one-sided, and where the original purpose of the stones was to assist the Earth now only the people were benefiting. There was an absence of real understanding and help for the Earth, and the end of two-way communication.

It is to their credit that only in recent centuries were the stones of the great circles stolen or destroyed, and they remain energetically in place today in the higher dimensions. The Earth exists independently of the stone circles, and its "organs" are still present under the stones. They continue to function, but it is easier for the Earth to function with your help. It's time to resume your part of the contract with the planet, and as the days approach 2012 this becomes ever more relevant. Stepping forward to help the planet is how you will help yourselves.

By maintaining many of the lesser stone circles in their fixed position across the globe there has been a small amount of harm done. Imagine having acupuncture needles left in your body after the treatment is over; it would do you no good and become a handicap. Only the great circles are in the correct locations and the rest have become redundant. For this reason we wish those of you who can see the ley lines and energy points of the earth to construct small temporary modern equivalents of the ancient stone circles. These could be made of small stones, sticks of wood pushed into the ground, or human bodies standing in the right places anchoring universal life force energy or Reiki. When these sites have been unblocked during a day or night, then continual monitoring of the ebbs and flows of energy is needed. If you unblocked one stagnant point in your own area you would help the overall flow. Some of you have the knowledge to do this immediately, and others can learn from them.

The next chapter continues the story of the great stone circles, their history, and the roles they have played for the Earth. Of all the ancient monuments left to us today by the Atlanteans, these are the only ones that will reawaken and resume their roles in the future of the planet. There are many small steps to take before Avebury and Silbury Hill become fully functional again. Whether these steps are in Britain or in a far country they will all help, and we will see that they happen in the right order.

Today many visit Stonehenge and Avebury and take away from them a small feeling of closeness to the Earth. Some of those who walk around Stonehenge are aware of the feel of the Earth beneath their feet, and it is one of the best places to enjoy the vastness of her energy. Feeling her energy helps you learn why it was a special site to erect the stones; it was so very long ago that they were raised there.

Section Four

The Stone Circles

13

DUE TO their greater knowledge, Atlanteans had positions of importance in these new countries from the moment they arrived. They were persecuted in Atlantis, but in the new countries they formed the government where they instituted many of the ancient forms of law you are familiar with today. They brought with them from Atlantis the 'Golden Rule'; to treat others as you would be treated yourselves, and laws of hospitality that are still followed. These few basic rules glued the societies together. They also brought a hard-earned wisdom about the dangers of abuse of power.

The villages contained everything that was needed to learn about life and how to find yourself as a part of the Creator. We angels have thought about what happened to you in Atlantis, and saw the harm that came from living in the cities away from the land. There is not enough bare Earth for you to walk on; your footsteps are muffled and you have no connection with her. A mother-child relationship exists between the Earth and all those who live on her, and it is harder to get in touch with her in cities. Because of this we are sorry to see so many of you living there now, with more moving to the cities all the time.

Other societies had developed separately depending on the continent on which they lived. Britain, Ireland and France had the largest number of Atlanteans arrive and integrate with their villages. They also had a unique pre-Atlantean culture (Celtic) that completely vanished with recent invasions, especially those by the Romans. This was due in great part to the deforestation of the land over the years as Roman armies passed through.

In *Planet Earth Today*, the Earth was introduced to you, to remind you of your contract with her for the game of life played here. Can you imagine living on top of a being that was more energetically fluid, and because of the easy flow of energy had vitality and health? She could alter a rain shower if it would be beneficial to let the rain fall in one place, or hold it back in another. Her volcanic hotspots were uninhabited, no one would dream of living where they would impede her release of energy. Today animals are prepared to leave the areas where she needs to adjust and shake, and you used to do this also.

14

WHEN DID YOU begin to forget how to live with the Earth? It wasn't only due to increasing numbers of humans; it was forgetting that you had a symbiotic relationship. It would never happen that a planet would take on a species and host it without this relationship. The experience of living together is a co-dependent one, where each is learning from the other. As one species advances, so does the other in accelerated growth. This is the pattern of your lives here with each other and with the other life forms on Earth, and it is lack of understanding this which leads to a feeling of disconnection and loneliness. No one has ever been as alone as you are in your incarnate lives on Earth today. You have also managed to concentrate fear and internalise it; we see it as a common trait among humans. Fear is something you have acquired that is not native to your original soul. You have learned to be afraid during your lives here, something that never happened in your previous games on other planets. Fear can be undone by hope.

The days of Atlantis were long, over so many generations that you would not believe us if you were to hear a figure for them. At this time you look back to the ancient poet Homer and the poems of the Iliad and the Odyssey, or ancient Egypt; only a few thousand years of recorded history. How can you imagine what your civilisation will be like after 130,000 years? How primitive your present lives will look to you then. One thing that is different now is that there won't be an island somewhere that advances without the rest of the world. All of you will progress together in the future as a family. There is so much of your history that has been forgotten, and so much that is wrongly interpreted.

The stone circles and the Carnac lines of menhirs were put there by people who could see the Earth's need for stones in those places. Acupuncture promotes healing in people by balancing energy flows in their bodies, and this is how stone circles help the Earth. Stone circles are Atlantean in origin and made with its lost knowledge, and helped the Earth by accelerating her growth towards light.

Following the downfall the Earth became more stable and she once again became a fertile home for humanity. Resentment faded, seasons stabilised and crops grew with regularity. Life was a little harder in the wider world than Atlantis, but it looked more promising to us. We had watched four previous soul groups ascend from this planet with the active help of the Earth herself. We felt you were back on track for human and planetary ascension.

All this was so long ago that you have no real memory of it, and what happened after the fall of Atlantis is clouded in the same mist that hides Atlantis from you today. Great things happened and are forgotten, they passed into myths and legends and now you have trouble believing they ever happened. But we remember.

The great stone circle of Avebury and nearby Silbury Hill in Wiltshire, England were early constructions by the Atlanteans, as was Glastonbury Tor in Somerset. These were built in response to the Earth's requirements, the stone enhanced qualities of the planet that were already there. Avebury holds the key to the life of the Earth; it's the engine that will drive the energy down the ley lines when it's re-activated. It needs connection with universal energy to start working, and is part-way completed and in the hands of humans who know what they are doing.

The Avebury Circle is the essential energetic site in the Western world; one day it will realign the Earth with her proper position in the Universe. Projecting out from this site are lines of energy that connect to every planet in the solar system and the universe. The Earth is slightly out of place at the moment due to her disconnection to the universe, and when she reconnects it will be like realigning a cog in machinery. This planet is not the only one out of alignment, and when everything in the Universe is realigned all will be quickly drawn back into the Source of all life. Avebury therefore has its time for full reconnection; it was designed for this and will be ready when needed.

The Earth is disconnected from her fellow planets because she is struggling to cope with hosting the human game. Where she was stable throughout four previous ascension games, ever since you arrived she has been careering crazily on a path where she is never in balance.

Avebury is circular because it has the ability to rotate in the higher levels, and it's a delicate piece of machinery on six dimensional planes that looks like a great golden structure of spherical machinery. It will create a tunnel of light that will draw the Earth upwards into her ascension. The idea of planetary ascension and the Earth fitting into her place in the universe is the same thing. When everything in the universe reaches either the extreme of dark or the extreme of light (level twelve on the ascension scale) everything will go back into the Source. Avebury was designed to assist the Earth to ascend to light.

There was a great crystal shaped like a flame the size of a multi-storey building on the top of Silbury Hill, close to Avebury. It focused universal energy and light down into the planet like a laser beam, kept the planet connected to the outer universe and allowed it to soak up the light of the stars.

In the battles with the former Eastern confederation, known in later years as the Shadow of the East, the crystal was thrown down and broken and its light was extinguished. Those living in the area that looked after the hill were slaughtered or scattered and there was a great break in the passing on of knowledge. Afterwards those who could remember some of the information continued their roles, but with diminished effect.

Humans built circles of stone and wood because those were the resources available for building in the physical dimensions. The great circles under the sea are far older than Avebury and far larger, built by using available underwater materials. They were put under the sea by sea-dwellers for specific purposes and safekeeping, and have purer energy than the land based circles. Sometimes the Earth has need of circles positioned in places other than dry land, and beings on this planet today other than humans make and carry out plans on her behalf. It's not just the humans who are considered important.

Glastonbury Tor rises high over the Somerset plain and is thought to have been the site of many historic places. One is the Vale of Avalon where King Arthur and Queen Guinevere are buried; another legend has to do with the Glastonbury Thorn growing from the staff of Joseph of Arimathea. The real significance of Glastonbury Tor lies not in its tower or its high mound but in the great seal buried at its base, and the true story of the Tor is far older than any tales now told on Earth. We'll give it a modern twist.

When the Earth was first created she had an escape button that she could activate if she felt that the game on her surface was leading her away from the light into darkness and if terminated, there was a chance that she could escape this fate. Remember that the Earth was willing to host these games on her surface to help souls ascend, and she would only want to terminate their game as a last resort. When the Earth first took physical form it was a bit like a new computer, built with many different ports and plug-in points that were surplus until needed. Many of these ports were energetically sealed, like a rubber plug over a USB port, until such a time when they were needed and the seal could be removed. For many ages, the Earth felt no need to activate her escape button and she purred along while the first four games were being played out on her surface. However, when she came to her fifth game, the Earth was gradually plunged into chaos being pulled this way and that by the human game on her surface, while suffering abuse. The first near catastrophe came in the last age of Atlantis, but the angels found a way to remove the problem and give the rest of humanity a chance to finish the game in light, rather than doom humanity to darkness because of the Atlanteans. The Earth agreed to this but in a 'they can have one more chance' way. But the darkness was not gone from the Earth's surface and trouble arose yet again.

The Atlanteans who survived Atlantis and made new settlements knew the importance of the seal to the Earth. (All the wisdom they knew that you have forgotten!) They built the Tor on top of the seal to protect it from the dark entities, who would have liked nothing better than to take control of it. If the Earth could not push it to save herself she would have to fall with her human population into darkness. This is why the last great battle of Arthur's time occurred over the seal at Glastonbury Tor.

This seal does more than provide an escape for the Earth, and because it has the power to terminate the game on the surface it also ensures the game continues. It contains in itself all the rules of the game on the surface, such as how time moves, what the atmosphere is like, how many dimensions the population can or can't see, etc. It also ensures that the population's experience of the universe is governed by these rules until they outgrow it; i.e. people can travel to Mars and will only see Mars in our dimensions, working within our laws of linear time. Any Martians living there may live in a different dimension using different time; therefore we would not be able to interact with their world or them with us, until one or the other progressed to a point where these divisions collapsed. This would happen when a soul ascended to light and merged with the rest of the universe. Every planet that is hosting a game has such a seal and it keeps each game on each separate planet self-contained with its own set of rules.

The planet's shield came forth from Stonehenge, circled the Earth and returned into a receiver on the opposite side of the planet. Stonehenge is the projecting side and the receiving side is the other side of the world under the ocean.

For millennia the shield had been dismantled and rendered ineffective by actions of the dark angels; ever since the destruction of Atlantis and the time of the new civilisations being established around the edges of the Atlantic Ocean. This meant the Earth was wide open, like a Wild West town without a sheriff. Angels of the dark orders flocked here and began mining the planet, for it was a place where they could all live undisturbed and where the pickings were rich. These dark angels were only able to strip the planet because the local soul group (humans) literally turned a blind eye. There was no resistance to what happened here. The shield is reconstructed now with the help of the angels of light, the Earth and some who have incarnated here to fight for her. It is this that gives us all hope for the future.

The Earth with her shield restored is a healthier Earth, one that has her first line of defence in place for protection.

This allows her to have a breathing space to remove anything that has come here to feed off her. This planet becomes clearer as time goes by and once the dark entities are gone it is difficult for them to return. While much has been done, there is a lot more to do to restore the balance.

The world is changing rapidly now with the help of humanity. If there was one thing that we would like to see all of you to do it would be to flow with all the changes happening everywhere. It is time for vast change to take place, and it is safe for you to go with these changes. What won't work for anyone is holding on and being stagnant. The energy of change does not support staying still.

All of the stone circles, large and small, that dot the surface of the Earth have been set there for a purpose and there is much speculation about them. It is not necessary for you to speculate as the stones themselves remember, and we who have been here all along also remember and have seen events unfold. The stone structures were built to promote health for the Earth, because a healthy Earth provides a healthy place for all to live.

We do not see you constructing any additional large stone circles before the end of your game here, for those days are past. We do see a new sensitivity to the flows of Earth energy that exist here already. Some of you are aware of the flow present through the lower branches of the trees at about the level of the upper deck on a double-decker bus; others are good at dowsing or seeing the ley lines on the surface as they run across the grass. Deep within the Earth is a network that connects to these upper lines, and far, far above is her energy body with its ebbs and flows. A flexible, comprehensive form of Earth healing is needed to help her, and there is nothing better than resuming the Reiki circles described in *Planet Earth Today*.

15

THE GREAT SEAL under Glastonbury was broken recently to allow the next phase of human development to take place. The rule of linear time was dissolved which kept time going forward in a straight line, and understanding the true nature of time will help set you free. Time, with its irregularities and flexibilities, is released from having to move in a straight line of cause and effect, and is now free to occur instantaneously. Every millisecond that ever occurred since the beginning of this planet is replayed simultaneously over and over, while at the same moment moving forward. All events occur simultaneously, thus the potential for events is increased a million-fold. Time is renewed every instant. The human soul group sits as a single entity throughout time; it exists in the timelessness of the universe. The time-lines on this planet used to be complicated enough, but now they are a million times more complicated.

The seal held the key to opening the planet to the universe, to align planetary time with universal time. The Earth can't continue to run on her local time and then rejoin universal time as a being of light; but the shift doesn't have to be instantaneous. You all have time to learn and adjust and go with her when she goes.

What does it mean to have everything happen at once? For a start it means that things that happened in your personal past can be released and discarded. Hurtful events can be let go and future worries released if there is no past and no future. What happens when you focus on the present where you are right now? Some of you have learned that being in the present is the only place you can ever be, neither in the past nor in the future. Others have settled into the present and found that it is the only place with real power of action, or just real power. What about forward planning? In the present you can plan for tomorrow, but when tomorrow happens it is the present. It sounds overly simple, but hardly anyone on your planet lives in the present. Most of you focus on the future or the past, and much of that is worry or regret. You only become one with time when you are in the present, and time is similar to watching a film as it moves past you while you sit still. Humans are contracted into physical bodies in a game that includes linear time, and time is part of the illusion of the game.

It is important to understand that you are always in the present before you can understand some further concepts. In a series of steps this is the first step, to bring one hundred percent of your focus to what is happening now in every moment of your day. It's actually a very large space, the present, and is the only space that matters in your lives. In the present and nowhere else, your lives are lived. Some of you will be better than others at focussing on the present, but all of you will need to practice it and bring your mind back when it wanders into the past or future. It's a good way to ground yourselves in your own lives.

Going over the past is something that everyone does, and when we tell you it does not exist you know it did, you were there and did those things, and knew people who have since passed on. This is not what we are talking about; we are talking about universal time, the overriding timeframe for the universe. When you are able to live in the now you have stepped higher as it were, left your planetary game for a moment and moved back into your universal home. It can be the place where you drop everything that bothers you as you spend some time as your real self. To let go and be the person who is the real you inside the personality you are accustomed to being. Finding yourself in the present provides moments of great relief and joy, to just be you without any extra layers. This core you is always present but so hard to find as an adult; it is worth searching for.

When you live in the present it is easier to find the light and the truth; mere glimpses at first, but the point of the present is that it is truth and the past and future are not. Some examples are "I'm afraid of what could happen in the future." This brings fear into your life today. "There was a cover-up in the past." You are hooked with grappling hooks into this past event, unable to live today. This is very basic instruction, so basic that we need you to practice it before you understand what happens when you are fully present in your life. We hope you enjoy releasing the problems associated with the past and future and living in the present.

16

THE GREAT SEAL of Time placed into the Tor at Glastonbury acted as a timer, and the breaking of the seal released the restrictions on time. It is a sign that things are changing, that time is no longer regulated. It was also the signal for many other happenings on the higher dimensional levels to initiate change. The end of time is the beginning of time for other happenings. It was a necessary first step, to allow the string holding the beads in a line to dissolve. With the string gone, natural order can resume and flexibility is restored.

Some of the changes about to take place will now accelerate. There is wide interest in 2012; when the universe will send a light bath for the Earth to help strip her of layers of old darkness and fear. That will be a time of accelerated change for the planet, but in order for human beings to take advantage of the changes they will have to enter into the flow of those coming days. Unpeeling yourselves from the past and future will help you take advantage of the amount of light that will be arriving that year. Some of you will embrace this and move forward without effort, and some will find it harder. We do not wish to discourage anyone who finds this a little hard to do. Whatever steps you take are good, just keep moving forward and don't compare yourself to anyone else. It is only stagnant, rigid, and unmovable energy that will do you no good.

Over the years there have been many mentions of Great Seals being broken on Earth with different effects. There were a number of these installed in the planet in the beginning to cope with the conditions humans made on their game. Some of these Seals seemed pointless to us, restricting as they did the flow of energy present. Every time a Seal has been broken there has been a loosening of the restrictions on this beloved planet, and she has evolved a little herself. Now more than half have been broken, and with each removal she has been able to energetically move a little more. It is not important for us to talk now about these other seals, if you understand about the Seal of Time you will understand that the others were also imposing false conditions. All the Seals will be broken before the end, and you will need to adjust to the new conditions as they happen.

It has been a long time since Atlantis was removed from the physical dimensions of the Earth, much longer than you think. One of the things that happened at that time was the cutting of Earth-time on each side of Atlantis, and that makes it harder for you to find or remember. You are entering a stage in 2012 that is as new to humanity as that morning when the Atlantean archipelago was removed forever and there was nothing but ocean waves where land had been. Of all the periods of time you can side-step to, Atlantis is the hardest for you to reach. Not impossible, but almost impossible. Yet Atlantis started a process that is still here, the echoes and events of the past are still part of your world today. For this reason we encourage you to embrace truth and love and light wherever you can find it.

Removing Atlantis from the memory of the human race was considered desirable to hide the "advances" made during the Fourth Age. Those who survived knew about the cloning and other atrocities but had no wish or technical knowledge to repeat those mistakes. They looked upon the works of their persecutors with justifiable horror and were careful to let those memories and that knowledge die with the continent. They had no desire to talk about such things once they had gotten safely away.

More recently memories of Atlantis have begun to surface, often in dreams or visions. There was never enough contact or discussion between your seers in the past to put together a coherent picture. Now you have a number of people remembering Atlantis, writing about it in books and on the internet and still the information is garbled. It is not a place you can travel to except in your dreams and visions, and is not accessible to humans. You are banned.

Now when you speak and write about Atlantis it is through those who can hear our angelic voices; through people who have cultivated their ability to channel. Channelling is not something freakish, or crazy as in hearing voices inside that tell someone to feel bad about themselves or harm others; our voices give information and speak of love. Love is our nature, our focus and our goal. We speak now about Atlantis because it is the one story you need to remember in order to learn from past mistakes. You have not really taken many steps towards cloning, but you are repeating the same basic errors. You do not believe animals have souls, many of you believe you have only one life to live; you have no remembrance of your divine purpose in living on this planet at all. You play god with the lives of "lesser creatures" who are trapped into being your experimental subjects and some of you are already looking forward to the day when cloning can help you live longer. Who are the people you trust with this life and death ability to clone? Very few of you even know the names of those working in this area of science.

Atlantis provided an insular environment for scientific experimentation, and in your larger world society you have the potential for far greater damage. Do not stand by unquestioning about what is being done, often with your tax money, behind closed doors. Do this not only for yourself but for all life forms.

17

THE MOST FAMILIAR stone circles are in Europe where the knowledge of how to build and energise them lasted longest. Because they were made of stone you can still find them standing up and down the British Isles and northern Europe, and once there were vast numbers of energetic circles in all the countries settled by Atlanteans. Stone circles are a European variation of these that help the surface ley lines flow. They are not the only way to unblock stuck energy, and we don't recommend constructing new ones today. Those days are past.

It is time for you to provide this kind of help again, but now the most effective way is for small scale temporary constructions that will only last for a season. If you are working with a group of Reiki people or other healers ask for guidance to be shown the places that need to be unblocked. These are in every country, and when you find one in your area you can sit or stand in a circle and begin to bring through universal healing energy through the middle of the group *with the intention that it will unblock and restore the flow of energy* at that point. Stay there until the group feels that it is finished. Sometimes a person will feel the need to add something, a stone or a stick pushed into the ground, or something else. This should be done by the person who can see what is needed, and must be kept simple. It must be done with understanding, not meaningless ritual, chanting or superstition. When the flow has been unblocked at that point there will be other points, and other days. You can't pin energy down, it's a flow.

There are those who can help you find these locations, who are able to read the land and see the energy flowing and above all see the blockages. Ley lines have different appearances and different qualities to their energy, some are softer and others have more focus, like a laser. The ley lines were once marked by lines of trees and buildings because the trees worked with the planet by drawing the energy straight up from the ley lines into their trunks and branches. The higher-level ley lines are supported across a network of tree branches. It's easier for the Earth to have the help of the trees, and up until around five hundred years ago there were those living in Europe who could see the ley lines and knew where to place the trees and construct their buildings. People planted trees to help the Earth; it was a well-known folk practice.

The Earth's engine under Silbury Hill, which will one day start and move energy through Avebury and the ley line networks, needs to have the lines awake and flowing, ready for receiving the energy. Energy needs to circumnavigate the globe quickly on four levels, deep, surface, tree level and high up in the atmosphere. By gathering at places you have been guided to and by following your inspiration for temporary constructions and by healing, you will alter the energy at that point. You will not always be working on the surface ley lines, but it is true they have the greatest number of blockages because they are so easy to obstruct. Tree planting is again necessary on the lines, and if a tree is planted it will be in the right place for years. There is no need to worry that it will outlive its usefulness, as that's impossible. We encourage you to plant trees for so many good reasons.

If you assist those among you who can see the ley lines in setting up new circles you can practice seeing them for yourself. All people can learn to read the flow of energy on the surface of the Earth as you did in the past, and never was there a more important time to resume this work. Many years ago the Atlanteans landed and monitored the energy flows in every country they settled and the Earth was stable, the seasons regular and predictable, and life was far easier for all. At this time the being who is suffering the most, and who is the most unstable is the planet. You are along for the ride and your lives are getting harder and harder as your climate becomes more extreme. If you begin to form healing circles, travel to various locations to unblock energy and help stabilize her you will be repaid with a return to balance. A few people doing this in one country are not enough. The knowledge of how to do this is present in many lands and cultures across the world, and does not have to be Reiki, although that is one of the simplest and effective. Look to your feng shui traditions to read the Earth and use the readings to balance the Earth before building a new building. That was the original use of feng shui. Lastly, you can feel it in your feet where the Earth needs help as you walk, follow your feet and you will usually end up in the right place.

We would see more of you put aside unimportant jobs and resume one of the primary duties of all humankind. It would be helpful to balance her, but always the main point of helping the Earth right now is to show her you remember your commitment to her, and are prepared to help and acknowledge her as a fellow being.

Section Five

How We Forgot the Past

18

WE ARE aware that you don't remember the Time of Legends, and no longer consider any of them real. It is popular to refer to the legends as mythological and to treat that time as something that never happened at all, was made up for entertainment, and told allegorical or teaching stories. There is a reason why this memory is so hard to access.

How long ago did Atlantis come to an end? When was Arthur the King of England? When was the last dragon seen? Whatever dates you name, they are guesses. An educated guess is still a guess. The answers to these questions are tied together with cause and effect, and are part of the long history of the human race. The downfall of Atlantis brought about such enormous changes in the Earth itself that everything was altered for the planet, the people, and all who lived on her. It altered the energy of the planet to lose part of herself, and it hugely interrupted the settled societies that were established on the surrounding continents. Imagine the shockwaves that went around the globe when Atlantis was removed; imagine the sorrow and mourning. There are still echoes of that sadness present here today.

To understand this you have to imagine what it's like to be an amputee after an accident, when you wake up and find part of yourself missing. The people who disembarked from ships after the catastrophe were in shock on many levels; they had seen the earth vanish from beneath their feet and the waves rush in. Many of their families may have died, and their trust in solid ground was badly shaken. They didn't know what was coming next, or if they could even trust the ground they walked on. They barely had any idea how to carry on living.

Their initial landfalls were wide-spread, and wherever they washed up they were met with help by elementals, the higher dimensional beings such as centaurs, dwarves or naiads, that lived in those areas. They were healed of much of their shock and space was made for them to live side-by-side with those already there. In time they remembered their culture and skills and built again the beautiful white cities of Atlantis, and this time there were no pits of darkness underneath. The cities housed only humans, because the elementals chose to live outside close to nature. Relations remained friendly between them and they were the early teachers on which crops would grow in the new lands and where to quarry and farm. The elementals assisted them in every way they could to help create a more positive energy to replace the sadness. When the Atlanteans were settled the elementals went back to their own tasks and lives. They co-existed for a long time before any problems arose. When they did it was a betrayal of the trust and kindness they had shown to the Atlanteans.

There was a wonderful period of time following the end of Atlantis when all the elementals were still visible to you; races that have since become invisible in your three dimensions. They live in your world, but not where you can see or persecute them. Unfortunately, they cast a spell so strong that they cannot reverse it alone. The day is coming when you will need to see each other again so that you can work together. It will not be much longer before some of you are ready to reverse this spell, but even then there are those who will never permit themselves to recognise what others begin to see.

After some time had elapsed the descendants of the original settlers began hunting the elementals, large and small, for sport. These beings are tied to the planet through love, and spend their time as caretakers and gardeners, although "gardeners" is too simple a term for their activities. The elementals were reluctant to leave the areas of their work, and were being destroyed because they would not run away. They took steps to protect themselves so they could continue to work for the Earth.

Even today you remember that fairies are magical. To use "magic" was to understand how to make things happen according to natural law, which in the decision to cast a hiding spell was mixed with panic. At the heart of their decision they knew that if they were killed the Earth would have no one doing their jobs of caring for her. They're not like us, not so blind and deaf. They took council together coming from many areas and representing all varieties of elementals. Many that came from the oceans are unfamiliar to us, as less is known about the deep sea than land. They emerged from the air, out of vegetation and rocks, and the Earth itself. In all their different forms and roles they joined together and agreed to go into hiding. With the Earth foremost in their minds they used their joint will to create a veil so that we would be on one side of it and they would be on the other. The veil came down to hide the fourth and fifth dimensions from humanity and we lost sight of them. Think of it as a bit like invisibility cloaks that hide them as they work around us.

The original veils were put here by the human soul at the start of your time on Earth, and it is possible for some of you to see through them. This is the only veil that was not designed by you as it would have made your stay here even harder. Once in place it changed the reality of your experience here, making it seem a much simpler world. You could not see the conscious life in the trees or flowers, or the souls of animals as you once did. You lost your heart connection to everything outside your own species. How much harder it became to learn about yourselves as part of a greater whole. This veil is removable, but things have to change first. Humans will be the ones to lift this veil when they are ready to see further, and with love.

In the beginning you lived among the three dimensions of height, width, and depth and the next two dimensions including time (fourth) and the elementals (fifth). Even saying this implies that there is a hierarchy and a separation. If we could name them after colours instead of numbers you would not rank them in any way, and like colours they can blend. You can see that the first three dimensions blend when you look around, and you do not categorise them into height, width and depth but see them as your whole world. The effect of having all dimensions in your lives would be to fill out and enrich your current world. The few places in this world that still have their higher dimensions are renowned for their beauty and beloved of the people who live near them.

Where these places exist the Earth has a full and open connection to the universe, and this is the underlying reason why these areas are considered so healthy and beautiful. Think of a doughnut hole in a ring doughnut, the hole in the middle allows the connection to be made to the outside universe and the planet to receive nourishment. When you visit one of these places and focus on the Earth you can feel the vibrancy of her, and this is how the entire planet once was. Full connection to the universe is necessary for planetary and human health and is what the elementals are working towards. They have some breathing holes, no bigger than freckles, and are always striving to enlarge them. Inside of these holes they are able to work as they originally intended. One day the Earth will return to health when she is fully reconnected to the universe.

How can you tell if you stumble across one of the Earth's breathing holes? The texture is richer; each leaf is distinct and can be seen from far away. Some of you will be able to see the elementals moving around, perhaps just out of the corner of your eye. It will almost always be in places where the land is cared for by the people who own the land, perhaps for generations. Or, in larger areas, countryside owned by families who love the land for its beauty and keep out inappropriate development. Beautiful public spaces are less likely to be these areas because of the absence of personal responsibility. These tantalising glimpses of how the entire Earth used to be when she was whole and undamaged also show you what we hope to see again.

These breathing holes have kept Earth alive over many years. They keep her from suffocating, and are maintained jointly by elementals and humans through love. They worked separately for the same end, to preserve something of beauty, whether spectacular, unusual, significant or surprising. The largest of these areas, the Lake District in Cumbria, England has been preserved by generations of local people who loved their land. It is one of the places where you can look down a valley and see the life and joy rising from the land itself, as every part of the Earth once was. What if, instead of working separately, the people had consciously worked with the elementals of the Lake District as they used to work together long ago? In this case love was enough, but in the rest of the planet the connecting places are smaller, and often uninhabited. Rather than rush to visit the Lake District, why not seek out places near you that you can love and protect, and rejoin to the universe? Some of you I hope are thinking about a place near you that may fit into the list.

Many of these locations are more fragile than the Lake District and do not need the crush of humanity visiting them. They are known to those living near them, and are protected by silence and love. What we see happening over the coming years is new places being created to connect to the universe, and smaller areas being enlarged. This will come about as humans learn more about how to recognise these places and take care of those already in existence.

The elementals work energetically and physically with the planet and their lives are entwined with the natural world. They each have their own energy, so a gnome carries different energy from a unicorn. The earthiness of the gnome allows it to sense any disturbance in the soil and rocks, and they are able to repair the energy of the earth where they live. By maintaining strength in the energy of their habitat they help the planet to stay strong. They've all had a hard time for millennia, working harder and harder to help Earth stabilise and keep her energy flowing. Unicorns protect beauty, innocence, and purity wherever they can. They have that long horn for a reason, and have a hard edge to their energy. Don't mess with unicorns! There are far more kinds of elementals than you have ever heard of, and the ones you come across in stories and pictures are just the tip of the iceberg. Those of you who find it easy to connect with elementals could help by learning from them how to care for the planet and putting what you learn into practice. Otherwise they are busy, stretched to capacity trying to hold the Earth together where she is most under threat from humans.

The effect of this separation between people and elementals was to cause a split in your perception of events that happen on Earth. While they are living in a whole and complete world of many dimensions, we are living in just the part we can see and hear. We are missing out on so much information that we cannot integrate our actions with the rest of the species or the planet, and we live alone and cut off from all other life. Our relationship with animals is not one of equals, but of food, servants and pets. We carelessly dirty and harm the planet we live on. Much of this was happening in Atlantis previously, but when the veil came down living with others was quickly forgotten. Rather than blame the elementals or humans for this turn of events, it is for both to work toward meeting again in the future. When you hear the phrase "the veils are thinning", this is one of the veils closest to you.

The veil was produced with a spell formed of will power and unified action, and it cracked down into place so life proceeded simultaneously on both sides of the veil. From that point onwards people lived at the level of a human toddler, cut off from knowledge and perception. Most people now don't believe in fairies etc., or in any kind of extra-dimensional sight or hearing. This brought about a different set of problems for elementals because they found they could not now undo the spell even if they wanted to. They're stuck on their side of the veil, and we're stuck on ours.

———————————————————

Above is shown two timelines; the lower one is the reality of a five dimensional world where much has happened, and still happens. The upper one is our perceived reality after the veil came down. They don't touch; it's as if two separate worlds exist at once in the same place. The complete world is the lower line, and our familiar world is the upper line. You can look all you want for the Time of Legends, but you can't find it unless you can walk in both worlds at once.

19

THE SPELL of invisibility was cast to exist as long as the Earth shall last. Elementals are higher dimensional beings, and sights of them today are through their dimensions, not through the three Earth-bound dimensions. Because some of you can see through into the higher dimensions and see them it means that every human has this ability. It also indicates that after a very stagnant, fearful time things are loosening up again and it is safe to see farther and talk about it. You will never go back to burning as witches those that have advanced sight. It is time now to begin to see again, because being veiled is not serving you as a soul group. Moving beyond the veils is part of your ascension process, and as you move from lower dimensions up to the highest twelfth dimension you will remember you contain your Creator within you. The twelfth dimension is divine. When you know that you are divine and return to light, you will have reached that dimension.

We as angels are doing all in our power to help humanity rise into the light, and we are not alone in this. It will become easier as more of you lead the way and see through the dimensions. Seeing into the higher dimensions begins when you acknowledge to yourself that it is possible, and then noticing the movement of other beings out of the corner of your eye. They are busy and there is a lot of movement from them, first see the movement, and then see who is moving and what they are doing. You may see them as colourless at first, and then find they have more colour and solidity as you practice. Finally a simple "Hello, I can see you." may start a conversation or get some attention focused on you. They are waiting for people to see them and help them with the Earth: you will make progress as you practice. Anyone who has chosen to read this book is ready to begin to see elementals.

What can you expect when you start to be aware of the elementals in your world? These beings are benign but harried with too much to do for the planet, guarding and balancing her. They are used to working next to you while you can't see them. They focus on her and are not looking at you directly; they ignore you. This changes when you look at them and address them directly. Your influence on the Earth, by your actions or failing to act, is so important that if they can teach you how to care for the Earth it will be the quickest form of improvement. Everything you wish you knew about healing the Earth of her hurts has been studied and discovered by the elementals already, and there is nothing they can't help you with. This brief period of humans beginning to see elementals, acknowledging their responsibility in fouling the surface and changing how to live, will not take very long. You will be able to see elementals in your next generation, and they will begin to help you then. There will be a return to the Earth of the days before the veil, and the damage will be repaired.

The effort to raise this particular veil and remove the spell will be enormous and will need to have enough people working together on just this one event to make it possible. What will be needed is a core of those who see beyond this veil now, and those who believe that it is possible. When the percentage is large enough of the total population then the counter-spell, the unity of focus and desire of a large enough group of people, will take place. Until that day no small group will be able to reverse this planetary spell.

20

WHEN THE day of united action and desire happens the veil will dissolve and disperse, it will be gone as quickly as it cracked into place and you will see your fellow residents of Earth. You will have the help you need to make important changes in living and in balancing and cleaning the Earth. Life is not all service to the planet for you as it is for the elementals, but it is part of how one lives with a planet. You will live more contentedly when you are in tune with your surroundings, and live in a healthy way. You each have a purpose in being alive here, and it is when you are working towards your goals that you are most content.

Elementals have a long history in this universe, and you will find them living and working on every planet and every star, except those they have had to vacate or die. They are attached through bonds of love to the larger being they serve and at times seem to be an extension of the planet. They are a separate soul group, and live in their own dimensions as well as yours. They are beings of light and have a great deal of strength they draw by living in a loving relationship with the natural world and the planet. They are hardy and have a great variety of shapes and sizes from the largest dragons on the peaks of the Himalayas playing with the clouds, to the tiniest water nymph sitting on a raindrop. They work so hard to maintain balance in the face of wanton destruction.

When you go with a group to focus healing energy on the Earth for her sole use, you will attract an enormous crowd of elementals. The most likely ones to come straight away are the divas, who have an organizing role. They are the ones who will notify others that they are needed and are very plugged into the needs of the Earth. They will probably call gnomes who work underground, centaurs who are healers, elves and fairies, dragons if the land is hilly, dryads in woods, naiads and water nymphs near water. Those who heal from boats in the ocean or on the sea shore will get a completely different group of unnamed elementals, although some of you have heard the mermaids singing and healing with their songs. The oceanic elementals tend to be much, much larger. Their world has been so ravaged by fishing and oil spills that their job is the hardest of all. In the air there are also many, from small ones who can sit on a leaf, to wispy floating ones cleaning and scrubbing the air. Just don't think these hard working beings can keep pace with the destruction humans inflict on the planet. They are never going to be able to clean it up without your help.

One of the most important things you could do is to plant more trees, and fit them in everywhere you can find a space. Trees support the energy skin of the Earth and there are deforested areas where that skin has collapsed. Other areas have only a few trees, and that is not enough either. Before there were so many of you cutting trees for firewood the Earth had less desert and more forests. This planet was designed to work with trees to support its energy, and it is another unseen loss when they are removed from the landscape. They hold the energy of love to remind you that there is love in the world while they help the earth. Lean against a large tree and sense the life of the many elementals living there, trees make a home for so many animals and other beings. Each one cut down removes this from your world and you become poorer by it.

Trees were used to make large circles in many places across the world in times past. This would be our number one preferred way of making any new circles. It will not always be possible to plant trees in circles so we have given you other, more temporary ways which will unblock the ley lines when you use them. If you plant a circle of trees it will make a connection point between the ground surface ley lines and the ley lines at branch level. The more connections between all these lines the greater the flexibility and flow of energy. The energy produced by the Earth's engine will be able to lift into the higher network of lines more easily to make the double-skin of energy stronger. The highest ley lines are being starved of energy, and assaulted by the imbalance in the Earth's atmosphere due to air pollution and the various kinds of radio waves you broadcast. Again, they depend on the health of the lines closest to the Earth. There are breaks in the deep ley lines below the surface, and they need the engine to restart to be helped more efficiently. There are crystals and elementals who work to keep those lines flowing.

When will the engine restart? Although the time gets ever closer, you need to do more work on the ley lines first. Would you fire up a power station when all the wires that carried the electricity away were broken down and hanging limp? It would do more harm than good. Don't wait for anyone else to start clearing ley lines, but go out with some like-minded friends and set up your healing circles. Take a picnic and enjoy yourselves being part of the whole world.

Section Six

King Arthur and the Time of Legends

21

THERE WAS a comprehensive split in time resulting from the spell to hide the Elementals from the Atlanteans. The real world continued on its way, while the new world of humanity continued in a narrower version. This is the world you live in, where animals and insects are your subjects, trees don't talk, and fairies don't exist.

How do you know about fairies, etc., when there is a huge spell and no one can see them? The effectiveness and thoroughness of the spell varied according to how strongly it was resisted by people. In a time when you would be burnt as a witch for seeing "something in the fire", and many were, those remaining did not have an open mind or talent to see. There were those who never saw, and weren't going to try if they thought it would lead to death. As the sightings died down (except among children), there was pressure to ridicule those who could see more than others. We say this to show you that you are different as individuals in your ability to see what lies beyond the three dimensions.

The following story is the most important of those that have been forgotten and considered as myth. It's a story about a time when there was an extra richness to life, and the world was more vibrant.

King Arthur, Queen Guinevere, and the wizard Merlin

Merlin was the first to incarnate, with the object of protecting Arthur when he was King so that he could do the work he came to do. Merlin was late Atlantean, in the sense that he was born in a time and place that remembered the skills of Atlantis in wizardry, and understood how to use natural law and energy to work with the Earth. He trained at the university at Avebury that passed on all the knowledge that was remembered about living with the Earth. Along with many others Merlin mastered the ebbs and flows of Earth energy; he could draw it to one place, or disburse it away, whichever was required for health and balance. There were many graduates who settled permanently near Avebury and worked with the energies of the great stone circles and kept them running smoothly. Merlin had the talent to learn all they could teach him, and he also learned from us, the angels who can still appear and teach when there is one willing to see and learn. He was as talented and as able as the best Atlantean wizards of the past, and learned much forgotten Atlantean lore by the time he was thirty. He worked with energy in a practical, hands-on way.

Merlin was around fourteen years old and Arthur about six when they first met. Merlin was able to look around and see where the energy concentrated, and feel the singular qualities of Arthur that let Merlin locate him. Running your fingers over a smooth piece of cloth with your eyes closed while feeling for one knot is similar to Merlin finding young Arthur by reading the flow of energy. Arthur and Merlin had agreed to incarnate and work together to avert a specific threat that would occur during their lifetimes. Merlin located Arthur and brought him to live at Avebury where Arthur also learned how to care for the Earth. Arthur was an adept pupil in understanding and began to look at what he needed to do to balance Merlin's work. As a small boy he did not remember clearly what he had incarnated to do in that lifetime, but with Merlin's guidance he was brought to us for teaching and we were able to help him remember. There wasn't much time left when Arthur incarnated as a small serious boy, very focused and quick to learn. We taught him so that he could begin his life's work from quite a young age.

The threat at that time was the Shadow of the East, the current manifestation of that Eastern confederation that was described as pushing on the borders of the North Atlantean civilisation. By Arthur's time the greater part of the post-Atlantean world had forgotten their knowledge and past, and there were only small areas remaining where some memory was retained. Egypt, Paris, the coastal cities of western France, Belgium, and North Africa held out the longest while the rest were conquered. Once they were overrun their culture was completely destroyed. Lives were lived with less balance and happiness, too many children were born, and they returned to the hard lives of farming. When the Earth is out of balance she does not provide rain and sun in beneficial amounts, and the inhabitants had ceased to care for the Earth.

Because Avebury was located in the island of Britain there was still a great deal of knowledge intact at the university and it remained a fertile and bounteous place to live. The pyramids in ancient Egypt stored universal energy to release slowly so there would be rain and sun in good measure, and similarly the great stone circles hummed with energy and dispersed it across Britain. The time came when the Easterners threatened Britain with their armies. This was before the births of Merlin and Arthur, who incarnated quickly to help keep Atlantean knowledge about the planet from being forgotten, and the world from being overrun by the enemy.

Arthur's story begins with the important figure of his mother Ygraine, who came of a long line of warriors.

Ygraine was the daughter of a great leader, a man tall and kingly, one of the last of the shining ones, and his head still glinted with the light of the unblemished sun present at his birth. He was born before all became dark, and at a time when generations had been keeping the darkness of the Shadow of the East at bay. In his lifetime the enemy was closing in and the light of the world was vanishing, the days darkened and everything went into a decline, into twilight. Ygraine was a war leader, wise and trained, young and strong. The people followed her to keep the enemy away from their city, which was a post-Atlantean civilisation of great complexity, culture, beauty and sophistication. It was situated where Brittany is today. At that time they were an island of light in the darkness and there was an unseen threat below the horizon.

Ygraine gave birth to Arthur because she chose to; she decided to have the baby and found a father for the inception. She knew who she was choosing to give birth to, and knew it was time to bring through this advanced soul.

Ygraine stood on her city walls and saw on the horizon the crackling darkness of the Shadow of the East, poised ready to wipe out the world of light. The enemy was far closer to her in Brittany than to the cities of Britain, and for her the sky had already turned to night. She could see the approaching danger and stood looking out with her little boy of four at her side. Arthur did not have time for a long childhood; he was trained in war by his mother and other war leaders. Ygraine's father and the men who served alongside her knew who Arthur would be and devoted themselves to training him in battle leadership. When Arthur was four they began their instruction and included him around the conference table as they made their plans for war. The enemy had come sooner than they had anticipated.

Merlin wrote to Ygraine and asked for Arthur to come to Avebury when he was about five or six. Merlin was eight years older than Arthur, and they were always good friends; Merlin the scholar, tall and gangly with a grin on his face, and Arthur the warrior. They learned by playing around at Avebury and being two boys learning by discovery and being taught by ourselves, angels of light. After eight years Merlin was 20 and Arthur was 12 or 13, when Merlin had to leave for a couple of years to complete a task elsewhere.

Arthur stayed behind and began to talk to the adults and teachers, who came to know him and gave him their full respect. Mature beyond his years, and wise with all he had learned at Avebury, Arthur had strength drawn from his close connection with the Earth. He was solid and balanced, and determined to protect what he loved. He made long-lasting relationships and gathered followers, and people began to know him and talk about him. Merlin returned to Avebury and they left together to return to France, and others followed them. Arthur began talking about fighting back against the Shadow of the East; he raised an army in France and united the remaining cities, while others raised an army for him in Britain. People were willing to fight, and they came together because of Arthur. He gathered the people together not only from Britain, but also from the nearby countries of Europe and he reunited what was left of the old North Atlantean civilisation.

This time had been foretold, seen in advance by the seers as a dangerous period when everything that was golden and lovely could end forever. Those behind the Eastern army drove their soldiers forward in fear and hatred, and they carried with them dark magicians who cast spells of destruction and painful death. Almost the whole of the European population was available to be drafted into the

Eastern armies. Their object was not balance and healthy living for all, but a recreation of the dark Atlantean days where fear provided food once more for the demons. Arthur knew what he was fighting for: the continuation of lives being lived with love and joy, and a planet that was appreciated and maintained in health.

A circle of Atlantean knights was founded who were trained in more than fighting. To be part of this circle a knight had to know how to heal and also spot the differences between those who were warriors for the light and those who served the dark. All of these knights were outstanding examples of the best a person can be in their lifetime. They were prepared to die to save the remaining Atlantean knowledge in the university and maintain the health of the land. As the years went on many of them did die.

Arthur's knights were drawn from each of the main cities in France, Britain and Ireland, and each city looked like it held a pinprick of light when its knight was home in residence. There the knights taught what they knew about fighting and healing to the cities' residents. At this time there was no sexist or ageist prejudice; a four year old child could be at the war table or a woman be a knight or war leader.

The names you remember these knights by today are not their real names, nor did they look like medieval knights of your world. They were Atlantean knights, shielded by protective energy like a force-field instead of metal. They carried their knowledge of energy as a weapon, and could erect an energy wall that would stop the oncoming army. They changed the flow and currents of the air to make the attackers' spears and stones from their catapults miss their targets. They could strip off the demons riding on the backs of the soldiers and banish them to the light. When the battles were over they were able to heal the Earth of her hurts by bringing universal energy through, and altering the flow of the energy under the ground to strengthen it. Only the most complete man or woman could be one of Arthur's knights.

You may imagine Arthur's capital city looked like a medieval castle with turrets, but it was an Atlantean city in appearance. It had white buildings made of smooth stone, in shapes that you would find unfamiliar today. There were elevated walkways and gardens, fountains and pools of water. Because the stones at Avebury look old you may think they lived in a primitive way, but that was not the case. It was an elegant life in beautiful surroundings. As in Atlantis, people walked when they wanted to go from one place to another, or they took the equivalent of horse-drawn buses for longer distances. Personal saddle horses were very rare.

In the early days Arthur had been given a sword, a stone and a crown. In a funny way this is partially remembered today, as the story behind "The Sword and the Stone", which led to a crown for Arthur. But the sword, stone and crown were our angelic gifts to him, as fellow fighters on the same side. We wanted to assist him in his life's work to keep the darkness at bay.

A long time ago the Archangel Melchizadek created the hallows, of which the sword, stone and crown were devised, that he used to help shape the Earth and lay the foundations for the physical presence here of humanity and other species of life on this planet. These were objects of power, and were entrusted to the Atlanteans in the earlier ages where each had a role and a place of use. When the Fourth Age was in full flow many of these were used for evil. They perished from the three physical dimensions of the world at the end of Atlantis, but their energetic presence remained in the higher dimensions. It was agreed to gift to Arthur the crown,

Excalibur the sword, and the stone. These were remade in the first three dimensions for him.

Arthur's crown had many properties and was a connection between him and the higher dimensions. It worked like a radio link to the angels of light, and gave him access to some of the talents he held in his higher self, the part of him that existed outside his body. An individual's higher self, or soul, is huge compared with the physical body. If you can imagine that you are so big that you can only fit your little finger into your physical body and the rest of your higher self has to stay outside as an extension of you then you have some idea of your true size. The vast knowledge and skills you have accumulated over lifetimes are rarely available to you specifically in an incarnation. Arthur was helped by the hallow that was a crown to access this knowledge. Other properties of the crown included a link to the Earth and to the higher dimensions. The Earth and the sky met in his person. The crown brought the knowledge of the universe to Arthur.

Excalibur is a hallow shaped like a sword, with the ability to slice through enemies in the higher dimensions. This was vital to Arthur as he could see both the dark entities and the humans controlled by them, and Excalibur would allow him to destroy the demon. It was far more than an ordinary sword, as it worked on levels not visible to most today. It is still feared when it appears in battles against darkness.

We gave Arthur the stone to keep him alive, a hallow of protection. This he wore for many years on a necklace under his shirt where few ever saw or noticed it. When the final battle came he was no longer wearing it, for he had given it to another.

Arthur was initiated as a priest in the order of Melchizadek, the same Atlantean order that contested evil in the Third Age of Atlantis. Those who are initiated as priests by Melchizadek are able to hold the energy of the hallows, and use them. By the time he was crowned king he was a young man of great energetic strength, one who had worked for the light actively and selflessly. He was entrusted with these hallows of great power and high vibration to use them as he saw fit. The hallows are neither good nor bad; they are able to be used for the light or against it and are not entrusted to anyone who may misuse them. We give them out now and again even today.

The crisis that Arthur and Merlin had incarnated to avert was fast approaching. It was so long ago now, but at that time there was an early chance to snuff out all that was beautiful and good on the Earth. If the Shadow from the East could conquer Britain and remove all the people who knew about loving and helping the planet, who recognised their role as partners with her in a reciprocal relationship, then the light of the Earth herself would vanish. With no light from her she would sink into darkness and wait for the end of the universe as a planet of misery. Everything that could be done to avoid that was put into place.

Arthur's base was in central Normandy where people came to join him from the remaining unconquered areas in Belgium, Brittany, Gascony, and other enclaves of light. He returned to visit the city of his birth. As Arthur walked through the woods one evening he saw a young girl dancing, a girl of thirteen or fourteen. He was not yet eighteen and was stricken with her grace and beauty. A girl of small stature, but irradiating light and strength like steel in the moonlight, this was Arthur's first sighting of Guinevere. He did not speak to her or call out to her that night but returned home to ask his mother if she knew who she was. Ygraine was pleased, because she could see Guinevere was royalty of an unusual kind, a sister (as all fairies are) to Titania, queen of the fairies. During all the years of her life, where Guinevere went the veil hiding the elementals was pulled up tight behind her and she had their support and company, although she had incarnated in a human body to play a role of importance for humanity.

Arthur left for battle without meeting Guinevere. Two years later he returned and looked for her again by moonlight, and called her name. She came to him, remembering the contract they agreed before they were born. Guinevere and Arthur married while still young, each afraid they may not have much time together if Arthur was not victorious. She remained behind when Arthur returned to battle and helped in her own way. She was often to be found in the forest, apparently sitting still and alone, but surrounded by her kin, while they worked together to strengthen the Earth. The young queen was honoured and respected by all the people.

Guinevere's role was to establish a bloodline that still exists on Earth today. There are many people who hold within a spark of light that can be fanned into a strong flame when they come up against evil. They live out their roles as protectors without knowing it, and have played important parts in the history of your present civilisations. Guinevere was as great a being of light as either Arthur or Merlin.

Guinevere and Arthur had one daughter, a young Ygraine who resembled her grandmother in many ways. She was raised by Guinevere and Ygraine from the beginning to be a knight, healer and warrior. Her birth marked the beginning of hope for many, although they did not know why. Arthur was away during her early years, and her training by her mother included the knowledge of the Earth that is shared by the elementals. From all the kindred of elementals information was provided for her teaching. She was strong like Arthur, but slender and small like Guinevere. She combined the best they both had to offer. Never before had an elemental incarnated as human, to marry a human, and it was done to provide this bloodline. Young Ygraine carried the love of the Earth in her genes. There was no veil for her, and she saw the planet as it really was. Later this was of great importance.

Arthur, Merlin and the allied armies fought for years and drove the enemy back into central Europe where Germany is today, they were making headway and gaining ground. France, Switzerland, and Spain were re-conquered and the light spread out again as the darkness was lifted. When they came to Germany the light began to be smothered as if with tar, and armies of good men were lost in the fighting. Merlin was surrounded in a forest by twenty or more dark wizards who ambushed him with spells of destruction. He fought back but in the end his body was dead and his soul had been cursed so that it couldn't leave for the higher dimensions. He was encased in rock like crystal and his soul looked out and struggled for years to get free. No one would go into that part of the forest afterwards where the remnants of the curses lingered. It became a dark and wild place.

Many years later the day arrived when a beautiful, shining young woman came to Merlin, Ygraine the warrior daughter of Arthur. As she walked through the forests looking for him she could see deeper than other people and saw the trapped soul of Merlin. Wielding Excalibur she cut him free from the spells. He returned to Avebury with her without his body, where some could sense him and talk to him, and some could not. He chose to stay in his Merlin incarnation working on the Earth, but without his body. He went to and fro repairing defences and putting up protection, and he placed artefacts in secret places where they could be found and used today. He did this because today is when the final threat is manifesting again, and the final battles will take place.

The allies lost two thirds of their knights and good warriors in Germany. They retreated in a direct line and returned to Britain through the Norfolk coast, when Arthur was aged about twenty-three. He put up his coastal defences, great walls of light drawn from the Earth and facing the continent, impossible to break through. Arthur knew at this point that they were in trouble, and that he would not be returning to Europe to fight again. There were a few cities on the continent that were holding out, but they were being passed by to go after Arthur with full force.

There were regular attempts by the enemy to cross into Britain with fleets and armies. Britain was not easy to conquer while the stones were active; as the land was strong herself it made it more difficult for the Easterners. In battles she contributed by calling up wind and rain to drive into the oncoming enemy; she was an active partner who responded when she was asked for help.

Arthur met with his knights and fellow leaders, and they debated possible solutions. The Enemy's goal was to wipe out Arthur and his army and take control of Glastonbury Tor and the reset button underneath; forcing the Earth to continue with a game that dragged her unwillingly into darkness. Arthur's knights engineered a trap around Glastonbury to draw the enemy into one place for a final battle. The enemy approached from two directions at once, from North Wales and from the south coast of England. In Wales a village of druids was slaughtered to the last man defending the beachhead. They had filled the stones and mountains of Wales with Reiki, pure universal life force energy. This energy slowed down the invaders' march to join up for the battle.

Arthur's trap was barely ready in time. An ambush had been prepared on the wooded slopes of Glastonbury Tor, and his armies encircled the invaders. They knew that they were not strong enough for a complete victory, but if they threw everything into the fight and drove through to kill the leader and his knights they could achieve a partial victory. They did not expect to come out of the battle with many men left alive.

During the battle Arthur fought at the front wielding Excalibur, surrounded by his guard of knights. They fought to kill all of the leaders, so that not one would be left alive. As the day wore on their numbers became fewer and fewer, as did those of the enemy. Guinevere had been given the stone of protection by Arthur; she had her own battle to fight at the gates of the royal city. This battle she survived, but Arthur died.

The sorrow over the young leader's death among those left alive was profound, and they buried him with simple ceremony. So many knights and soldiers had died that day, and across the land the invading armies had destroyed the beautiful Atlantean cities as they had done in Europe. Survivors returned to the families and homes they had left so many years before. Devastation was everywhere across the land and few houses were left standing. The battle of Glastonbury removed the armies and threat of the East, but the great civilisations were gone, the people slaughtered and their wisdom for the most part lost and forgotten. The university at Avebury was destroyed, as were all the centres of learning. The populous and elegant cities became small villages, as you now imagine rustic villages in the past to be, and children were told tales of King Arthur and the legends of a forgotten time.

22

WHAT IS THE explanation for the events at the battle of Glastonbury Tor? Arthur was a warrior and champion for the Earth, while Guinevere was a healer laying plans that would outlast the final battle.

Arthur knew by the time he retreated to Britain that he would fail to re-conquer the European continent or be able to roll back darkness from the land. He was cornered in Britain and would have to make his last stand there with his army. The army was still large enough to put up a good fight, and before it could be whittled away by attrition and small battles Arthur needed to find a solution. He planned to ambush the Easterners on the slopes of Glastonbury Tor, towards which they were heading anyway. Great earthworks were thrown up, and the best defences that he could devise. He knew that if he removed the leader of the Shadow of the East, along with all his captains and knights he would remove the threat that Atlantis continued to face.

The Atlantean threat at the time was due to the advanced knowledge carried by both Arthur and his knights, and more destructively, by the Enemy and his captains. The Easterners were being driven forward by one man with his dark knights, who were also dangerous and skilled men. He was a cruel man, descended from good Atlanteans who settled in Europe many generations earlier. The angels of darkness taught him and he turned away from everything good while resurrecting many of the dark practices from the Fourth Age. He incorporated Atlantean knowledge, but twisted it for his own ends so he could rule everywhere. At that time the memory of how life was lived in Atlantis showed him that he could do anything they used to do in the past. He began when he came of age by overthrowing the dynasty that had built the Shadow Empire and taking it under his totalitarian rule by use of sorcery. He attracted those who enjoyed ruthless power and they became his captains. He built his armies and proceeded to wipe out everything of joy and light, and created an Empire of unhappy slaves. The knowledge of his invincibility through magic kept everyone docile and enslaved. Arthur incarnated as this man took power and made war on the lands that were still light.

On the other side the Atlantean influence on Arthur was of light and integrity. What you would call magic was an understanding of fundamental natural laws. He worked with the Earth and her flows of energy in a synergetic relationship; they worked as one. In the areas where the Shadow had not yet come there was a natural life, closer to the Earth, with the elegant Atlantean cities as regional centres. It's hard to imagine healthy crops leaping up out of the ground overnight, but this is what happened and these former Atlanteans knew it could happen this way. They lived pleasant lives and remembered their kinship with each other and true origins as people of a single great human soul. The sky at night was filled with the moon and friendly stars, and the darkness held no fear; it was an opportunity to walk outside and commune with the half of nature that was asleep in the daylight. Arthur drew to him knights who were adept in all the natural magic they needed to help sustain beautiful and purposeful lives.

When the original island of Atlantis was removed there was a compromise; she was willing to endure the pain of removal to give the non-Atlanteans living on other continents a chance to live and remember their purpose in being here. The problem by the time of Arthur was that the Atlanteans had become corrupted once again in their new civilisations. The Shadow Empire strove to turn the world black with fear. When all was dark except Arthur and his remaining army the Earth herself was trying to reach the termination button on her back to stop the game. The angels and mighty beings of light (Arthur and other living Atlanteans) pleaded for the human race and came to an agreement with the Earth that if all of those of Atlantean descent and influence, good and bad, died at once she would not reset her being for a new game. The powerful black and white pieces of the chessboard would be gone. There would only be the little pawns left from whom we are all now descended, including past civilisations of magic and slavery like ancient Egypt. Over and over in this game the Earth has had to endure the pain inflicted by the stupidity of human beings. Imagine a caveman with his club just hitting things with a stupid look on his face and that's the human race. Earth helped four races to ascension and remained stable throughout that time. Since you have arrived she has been careening crazily on a path where she is never in balance. The blood of the Atlanteans was the price for not ending the game at that time.

Arthur was facing the loss of the Earth to darkness, to the point where the game was lost and the human soul was trapped on the planet in misery until the end of the Universe (*Planet Earth Today Section One.*) The Enemy was heading straight for the reset button under Glastonbury Tor, and if he could possess it the Earth would be prevented from reforming in a way that did not support human life. Arthur was determined to keep the reset button protected for the Earth to use herself to honour the human contract with the planet. He also needed to remove from Earth those who could remember Atlantis, who had Atlantean knowledge as taught by angels of light and dark so long ago, and the threat of this knowledge ever again being used to harm the planet. His plan was to sacrifice himself, his knights, and all remaining men and women who remembered the Atlantean ways. At the same time he would destroy the leaders of the Shadow of the East, all captains, sorcerers and men of dark Atlantean knowledge.

Arthur laid his plans for ambush and went into battle holding nothing back, without reserves. He had no intention of living beyond the day and he drove straight through to the very centre of power and fought with the Enemy himself. His knights fought the captains, and Merlin's former students assisted by fighting the sorcerers and anyone who cast spells of dark magic. At the end of the day the Enemy had fallen to Arthur and Excalibur, and all the captains, knights, and wizards were dead. At the very end, Arthur let go of his own life and died. Most of the foot soldiers were dead, and those of the enemy who lived past the end of the battle escaped joyfully for home, no longer slaves.

(Note from the Angelic authors – We want to emphasize that our concern was/is the planet. We were ready to pull the plug on this game ourselves. The fact that we did not is down to the greatness of Arthur and his knights; true beings of light in every sense of the word. Arthur's sacrifice finally brought to an end the threat of Atlantis. Much that was good perished to get rid of the dark. We are still greatly saddened over the death of Arthur. He deserves to be honoured by all alive today.)

The name of Atlantis could never wholly be erased but all that was learned there about your role in the Universe was forgotten. It was as if a race of kings had come to an end, leaving the people behind leaderless. Very few soldiers returned to their homes after the battle from either side. Arthur, Merlin, Guinevere, Excalibur were remembered through fireside tales, and never forgotten although it all happened so long ago.

Arthur had to die to remove himself and his Atlantean knowledge from the planet: he was the last Atlantean king.

With the teachings and influence of the angels removed the journey humanity had to make was going to be slow, very slow with each step taken in correct order to fit into linear time. All those present here of the light and dark fraternities are also in the slow lane, taking one step after another with humanity. One of the effects of the battle of Glastonbury Tor is that this battle is unfinished and both the light and the dark were losers. The resulting stalemate is a lull in the fighting, and Arthur's final battle is unresolved. His story has never been forgotten, for it is unfinished and continues to be told in different lands and in different forms. We are still living in a world where Arthur's final battle is one of the most formative events in our lives, and we all have the memory of Arthur in our consciousness.

Arthur incarnated at a time when he had a chance to make a difference to the outcome of the battle for Earth. The confederation of nations that were lapping at the edges of the North Atlantean civilisation had consumed those lands over time. Those who lived there in harshness and slavery no longer remembered anything of Atlantis except the name. They did as they were told, and the Earth was despoiled. Arthur fought for the light, he fought to keep joy and love in the world. By his compromise he stripped out the best of the light and the worst of the dark. What remains today are both in diluted form and the final battle will be to either remove the light or remove the dark. At that time the battle for the Earth will have ended.

23

THERE ARE many stories about rings, magic rings, and rings of power. Many of these are part of northern European folklore and mythology recounting tales about their Gods and their struggles for power. Richard Wagner combined these stories into his operatic Ring Cycle, and J.R.R. Tolkien created a world where the Ring of Power plays a crucial role.

Wagner's Ring Cycle and Twilight of the Gods

In *The Ring Cycle* by Richard Wagner the ring begins as golden stones in the bottom of the Rhine, protected by the Rhine maidens; these stones are part of the Earth. An evil dwarf steals the stones and forges a golden ring of absolute power which he wears. The plots of the operas revolve around who can possess this ring and use its power. In *Twilight of the Gods*, the final opera of the Cycle, the ring is won back by one of the evil Nibelung dwarves, the son of the maker of the ring. At the end this dwarf is dragged by the Rhine maidens into the Rhine where he drowns. They reclaim the ring and restore its power back to the Earth. The music changes to show the earth and sky, river and mountains are united again. They assume their original shape and are linked according to their original natural order. But the beginning and the end have altered; the gold shines again in the depths of the waters, but in the memory of mankind the ring does not return completely to its former state of nature. It carries the knowledge of its creator, and the causes and consequences of the curse of the dwarves.

What was this ring, this ring of absolute power? It was the power of the Earth itself, stolen and forged into a ring that gave power to the wearer. The wearer abused the power of the Earth and did not consider her in any of his plans or activities. The power being transferred to the ring forced her to lie powerless and unable to regulate herself, or defend herself. As the operas progress and there are killings over the ring it is seen that there must be one who will come as a hero and retrieve the ring and destroy it, whilst not being corrupted by it. Wotan, the king of the Gods, deliberately breeds the hero Siegfried, and with Brunhilde he recovers the ring and is involved in its return to the Rhine.

The Rhine maidens receive the ring for the Earth and immediately natural order is restored, with sun and rain, and gentle winds bringing bounty to the planet and those who live on it. Disrupting the power of the Earth has led to unnecessary death and tragedy. In the end the Gods in the operas paid too heavy a price to own the ring and build their heavenly city of Valhalla. The beautiful city of the Gods has led to moral bankruptcy and, by removing them from the Earth, disconnection from the land.

This is an allegorical story about abusing the planet you live on, and how hard you can make it on yourselves by upsetting natural balance. The operas were written more than a hundred years ago and like some other stories were planted at the time of writing to be relevant today. As the end becomes closer and you approach the point when you will rejoin the universe in its timelessness, these tales are here to help you and will repay your contemplation of them. There are many more of these stories you can find in works of fiction and folklore.

This world was understood by Tolkien, who wove it into his beautiful fictional stories of bravery and courage, loss and struggle. Tolkien brought back into human consciousness some understanding of what it was like to live in the world while Arthur was alive.

24

J.R.R. TOLKIEN was familiar with the myths and legends of Europe; he felt the modern world was missing something by not having their own mythology and being unfamiliar with the old stories. In a wonderful life of creativity he wrote *The Lord of the Rings*, *The Hobbit* and *The Silmarillion*, etc. It doesn't matter that these are fiction because he wrote them so well as to give you a feeling for how the past could have been. Importantly, he saw the light and the dark in a way very few have since the fall of Arthur. In all your stories of angels there are very few about those who see the armies of the angels of darkness. These armies existed in a more physical form in the past as the Shadow from the East.

At the time of King Arthur the armies of darkness were as visible as the armies of orcs are in Tolkien's books. When Arthur's mother Ygraine stood on her city walls and knew the armies were just below the horizon, coming for her city and culture, they were real armies and she knew what they were like. Tolkien's description of the orcs, their appearance and their cruel societies, was a fairly accurate representation of the spirit of those armies. They looked like that to us although they were armies of men.

The creation of the world through music in *The Silmarillion* (*The Ainulindalë*), where the planet is more vibrant, more *whole*, because of the inclusion of harmony and disharmony, illustrates the true relationship between the light and the dark. Tolkien also wrote of Numenor and its fall, which captured the feel of the fall of Atlantis and the establishment of the North Atlantean civilisation without being factually correct. (Ygraine's father in Normandy looks like one of Tolkien's men of Numenor, born before its fall and who had once lived in a blessed realm.) The Atlantean knowledge marked the survivor's civilisation apart in much the same way as the newly established Numenorean kingdoms in Middle Earth. He took the story of the Ring of Power and fleshed it out so that readers could understand the characteristics of the angels of darkness.

Throughout *The Silmarillion* and into *The Lord of the Rings* you have characters that are adept at lying and deceiving those who listen to them. Sauron appears in both books as one who manipulates others with lies, and he convinces many to serve him and promises them rewards. His rewards are never what were promised. All the rings he makes and gives away twist the owners towards evil and joylessness. The owners become slaves themselves to the power in the rings. This is so important, by being slaves to power, or gold or anything that is not love and joy; human beings come to resemble the demons who told them the lies in the first place. Humanity has its own innate capacity for evil that can be brought forward.

The Atlantean themes run through the story of the Numenoreans, their blessed life in Numenor, and how it came to be a place of horror with human sacrifices. They lost their land when they attempted to conquer the undying lands where the Gods lived, and a few survivors washed up on the shores of Middle Earth. As with the cloning in Atlantis, they had fallen for lies that made them fear death. The Numenoreans never really rid themselves of this fear, even when they set up their new realms in exile in a land where their life span was so much longer. It was a fear that sat in dark corners and ate away at their civilisation. Their dead ancestors were honoured above the children they failed to have. It changes only at the very end when the king returns to the city in victory.

This overwhelming fear of death remains with you today. You do not see it as part of your greater cycle of life, as the beginning of the next phase of existence. There are those that long for death because their bodies are worn out, and there is nothing more natural than dying and crossing from life to death. They are two halves of the same coin. When you are dead you wonder why you struggled so hard to hang onto life. We see this worldwide fear, and know that fear is the way the lies get a toe-hold in your lives. If we could see this fear gone, to be replaced with acceptance then there would be a dark cloud lifted from the entire planet. All of you would sleep easier at night if you weren't afraid of dying. Remember the bigger picture explained to you in *Planet Earth Today* and allow death to arrive in your lives as a natural consequence of living.

The Downfall of the Lord of the Rings and the Return of the King

This is the title that Frodo gives his manuscript at the end of *The Lord of the Rings*. We are reminding you of Frodo's title here because it lost a little something when it was shortened. There is more balance in the long title, the Lord of the Rings versus the King. They are polar opposites with all of humanity in between. It reminds you that in the end it is not enough to remove something destructive, but it must be replaced with something good that will restore natural order. In this case it was Aragorn and he was the last king of the old days. His reign was followed by the modern world of men.

Sauron's ring, which would give him the power to conquer absolutely the remaining people of Middle Earth, had the same effect as the ring of the Nibelung. Tolkien describes the damage done to the living Earth of Mordor, and Saruman's destruction of the orchards of Isengard. Orcs crush the living plants with iron-clad feet, and in all their orc-talk there is an absence of love for anyone else. Sauron hopes to conquer all, as hobbits living as slaves in misery would please him more than hobbits living happy and free. Peter Jackson's *The Lord of the Rings* movies help us to visualise those who were aligned with Sauron.

King Arthur faced a threat as great as that of Sauron's army in *The Lord of the Rings*. When you think of the Shadow of the East, think of the men who marched to join Sauron, not the orcs. Arthur and Merlin stood in the position of Aragorn and Gandalf and looked at a sea of enemies blotting out the light of the world and knew they were making a final stand; none would gather the strength to fight again if they lost. Like those fictional heroes Arthur fought until he found himself at the last battle.

Tolkien writes that the final battles of *The Lord of the Rings* and *The Silmarillion* result in an older age finishing and a new age beginning. We like the way he captures the feel of the way things have been happening on your planet, when the elementals created their veil, and following the death of Arthur new ages on Earth were begun. There will be only one more change of this magnitude, one final age when conditions change again. We write because we want the change to be full of light, and full of love and hope.

The alliance of elves and men, dwarves and hobbits stood to lose everything, and they were prepared to fight the Enemy to the end. A similar alliance exists on Earth today, with men placed on both sides of the battle. Men have always been free to choose their path. Our role is to illuminate the pathways so they are clear and the price and destinations are plain to see.

Arthur's unfinished story has been told and retold in book after book, it is the story that we, the Archangels of Light, most wish you to know. It sits above your world as part of the akashic records of events, and it will be completed soon. Where he fought an army as overwhelming in every way as Sauron's you will also have your battles to fight. The goal is the same, to capture the ring and dissolve it back into the earth: to fight for the planet and recreate natural balance.

There are many problems you have on Earth today, and they are going to get worse as the damage you have done to your planet really starts to kick in. Some people will be waiting for another hero to save them like Frodo, but the real lesson to learn is that just one person can make a difference. You can make a difference.

We look and see those today who are as strong and dedicated as the heroes from your past; you have no shortage of heroes at this time. Natural balance, when the Earth provides rain at the right time and in the right amount, sunlight and shade, fertility and bounty, returns when she is a partner instead of a servant. This is a two-way relationship between two souls living together. When she is acknowledged she can choose to respond with balance again as she did in Numenor and Atlantis. King Arthur was the last hero who fought for her and for you, and to have this game end in light you will need to act yourselves.

The history of the human race includes reaching the highs and lows in lost Atlantis. So much was learned that has been forgotten; but it is time now to remember. It is time to remember what every Atlantean knew in the beginning; that they lived by arrangement with a living planet, that with her co-operation they could have rain and sun in moderation so that their lives were easy. When they allowed themselves to be tricked out of honouring her and caring for her in return they lost everything.

What they said about
Planet Earth Today

The clearest message for me is: We have to act now! This book suggests gentle, effective ways to make small changes in our daily lives and help secure a bright future for humanity and for the Earth that hosts us.

Deb Hoy, *Editor Touch Magazine. UK*
(available from www.reikiassociation.org.uk)

This clearly written, cleanly channelled book is a must for anyone willing to look at the bigger picture of Earth's history and humanity's part in her destiny.

Kristin Bonney, *Reiki Master UK*

"I have just begun on my Reiki path, and I am so moved by your work. Although I am new to this particular energy work, I have been involved in "alternative spirituality" for all of my adult life. I was particularly taken with the idea of having a healing circle for Gaia. When I first read about the Atlantean circles, I knew it was something I need to facilitate.

Thank you for bringing this fascinating work to light and inspiring me to take my life to the next level. I have already incorporated some of the core ideas into our drum circle and the women's circle. I want everyone to read this book and I will recommend it to all of my kindred spirits, and especially for the Gaia circle."

Karen Tlusty-Rissman, *USA*

Planet Earth Today

I am a teaching Reiki Master who studied for 10 years before being initiated in the Usui Shiki Ryoho Reiki system. During the course of the nineteen years I've been practicing my own Reiki, my ability to channel became clearer and stronger until a couple of years ago I realised I was able to see the world around me in a way that others were not. The world became populated with elementals, angels and demons; and visions of other times and dimensions. My efforts as I worked with my own archangelic guides was always to unblock and be clear, with no preconceptions of what they may say next; to stand well back and just watch and listen. My guides introduced me to certain people they wanted me to 'fast track' where they could answer all questions immediately through channelling, so these people could be ready to play their roles now and in 2012. These people would then move on and begin their work for the Earth.

Last year the Archangels wanted to write this book about the Earth, and because of the closeness of 2012 they wanted to shine a light into the dark corners and help us to see the reality of the world we live on. The book shows a sentient planet of incredible beauty, and a human soul of light that is under attack, lied to and deceived. I felt that as long as I was learning new information when writing, information that I couldn't begin to make up, I was on track as an accurate channel. They dictated this book, which was a combination of them explaining and me questioning. We collaborated, and I would say that seven of us wrote it together. Planet Earth Today is the first of the books that the Archangelic Collective are intending to write over the coming years, and they have much more they want to teach us. The contents of the books will always be relevant to what is happening at the moment of publication.

There is one story, a golden book like a long scroll and the two books I have completed have been lifted from here and typed up. I watched the flow of golden words enter the computer until suddenly it was the last page and the book was finished. After that my daughter and I checked and checked that I had got it down right, each paragraph and line examined to see if the golden energy ran through it steadily or if it wavered indicating that it was not quite accurate. Only when we were happy was a section considered complete. Later sometimes I would add to a section more clarity, as my own understanding improved and I could put in more detail. One of the very last paragraphs written was about the poor creature in the mines of Atlantis, and I think earlier I was not brave enough to watch his pain. I channel using a combination of sound and sight, whichever is quicker, and where it is written the best I have been writing down their words.

Sometimes it is the right time for a book to be written and read.

Contents of *Planet Earth Today*

Lightning Source UK Ltd.
Milton Keynes UK
UKOW051844081011

180003UK00001B/2/P